Our Heroes

Kids
Follow in
the
Footsteps
of the
Past

translated by Aviva Rappaport

Illustrated by Yoni Gerstein

Our Heroes

Chaim Walder

Originally published in 1998 in Hebrew
as *Yeladim b'Ikvot He'avar*

First published 1998

Copyright © 1998 by
Chaim Walder

FELDHEIM PUBLISHERS
POB 35002 / Jerusalem Israel

200 Airport Executive Park
Nanuet, NY 10954

10 9 8 7 6 5 4

Printed in Israel

To my beloved parents,

ר׳ שלמה ומרת פנינה ולדר שיחיו

to whom I owe everything

הועדה הרוחנית לבקרת ספרים
שעייי ביהייד של הרב נ. קרליץ

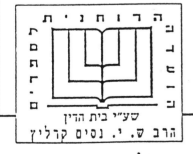

בס"ד יום שלישי

הנני אושר לציין הוצאה לאור של
הספר "ילדים בצדקות הזמר, ועתו אווות
בשר ותווי לקריאה.

מחבר הספר השכיל ליצוק בעובדות
סיפורין ערכי היעק ומוסר השכל בנפש בני הנוער,
ויש בספר זה תועלת רבה לחינוך בעיצות וטובבת
תורה.

וראוי כל מוסקים דרננו הספרים, להגיה, וללמדו של הצעיר
לדור צאו הרב לגבלות את הדרים דרכבית לאורים.

נ.קרליץ

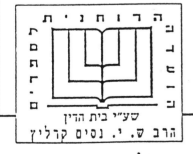

שעייי בית הדין
הרב ש. י. נסים קרליץ

טלפון 570 0419.

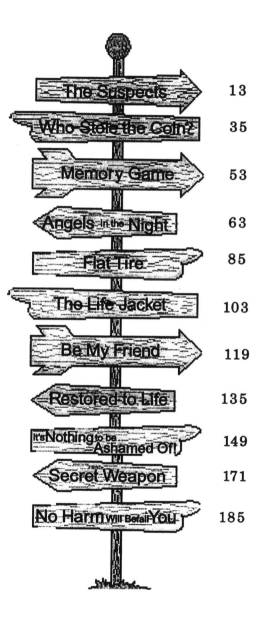

The Suspects

Yochanan's Story

The Suspects

I'm considered a pretty friendly kid...and a little bit mischievous, too.

To tell you my story from the beginning, I have to go back to a year ago, when I was in Rabbi Cohen's sixth grade class. He was a great teacher and also very nice. We all liked him a lot.

One day, in the middle of the last class, the teacher called on Yair, the boy who sat next to me. He was class monitor then. The teacher gave him a key chain full of keys and asked him to bring a certain notebook from the teachers' room.

Yair went, came back, handed the notebook to the teacher, and sat down. The class continued as usual, without any special interruptions.

At the end of the day, the teacher went over to Yair and asked him for the keys. Yair reached for his belt loop, where he had stuck the keys, but...

The belt loop was empty. The key ring had disappeared.

Yair started looking next to his desk. A few other boys helped him but the keys were nowhere to be found.

"Maybe you lost the key ring in the hall?" asked the teacher.

"I'm positive I didn't," answered Yair. "I remember having the key ring when I sat down. Yochanan even jangled them."

"Aha," said the teacher. "Yochanan, is that true?"

"It's true," I admitted.

"Then maybe 'by mistake' you also took them?"

I felt myself blush. "I didn't take them."

"You touched the keys so that they would jangle?"

"Yes."

"Why?"

"Because. Just for fun."

"Maybe you tried to take them and that's when they jangled?"

"I didn't try to take them."

"Yochanan!"

"I promise! I only jangled them for fun. What am I — a thief?"

"You're the one who said it. I'm just looking for my keys."

One look at Rabbi Cohen's face told me he

didn't believe a word I said. I felt terrible. I knew the truth — that he suspected me for nothing. I had no idea where the keys were.

"Bring me your briefcase," he said.

I brought him my briefcase, with the eyes of half my classmates following me.

The teacher started to search through my things. The keys weren't found.

"Where are the keys?" asked the teacher. "You'd better tell me and be done with it."

"I don't know. I promise I didn't take them," I said. I felt like crying, but I didn't because I was too embarrassed to cry in front of my friends.

"Then why did you touch the keys?"

"No special reason. I just wanted to hear them make a noise," I said.

The teacher looked like he didn't know what to do next. You could tell by the look on his face that he didn't believe me.

But it was the truth.

I collected my books, put them in my briefcase, and left, leaving the teacher and Yair behind, still looking for the lost key chain.

As I walked home, I thought hard. I knew the teacher suspected me of taking the keys but there was no way I could prove to him it wasn't true. And I didn't know what to do about it.

Little did I know my troubles were just beginning. That night, at home, the phone rang in our house. It was the teacher. He told my parents what happened, and they started asking me questions. I denied any connection to the disappearance of the keys, but they didn't believe me. Mostly they stuck to the fact that I had jangled the keys. They reasoned that it was undeniable proof that I wanted to take the keys.

"Look, it's no joke," my father said. "Your teacher is very worried. Those keys are the keys to his house and the school. He said that if the key chain isn't found, he'll have to change all the locks. Don't be stubborn. Tell us where you hid them."

I didn't have any answer. I had already said everything I could to deny it, so I just kept quiet.

My parents called the teacher again. It sounded like they didn't know what to do. At the end of the conversation, my father came over to me and said, "I have a suggestion as to how you can get out of this honorably. Tomorrow, go to school about ten minutes early and put the key chain on the teacher's desk. That way there won't be any problems."

"But I don't have the key chain," I protested.

"Did you hear what I said?" my father said.

I went to bed.

For some reason, when I woke up the next morning I forgot about the whole thing. I went to shul to *daven* and from there, I went straight to school. That was when I first remembered what had happened the day before. Suddenly I didn't feel like going any more.

I got to class several minutes late. I walked in hesitantly. The teacher was standing near the door. He looked at me and whispered, "So, you finally got smart."

I didn't know what he was talking about.

"You accepted the suggestion I gave your parents to put the key ring on my desk. As I promised them, I will not punish you. But I am interested in knowing what would make a boy like you do such a shameful thing. What did you hope to gain from it?"

Those last words were heard by a few of my classmates who sat near the door. I turned beet red.

"It wasn't me who put the keys on your desk," I said.

"Come on," said the teacher, "do you want to start this all over again?"

"I just got here from shul and—"

"Sit down. It would be a shame to get caught up in it again," said the teacher.

I sat down, feeling more and more furious by the second. I realized that the teacher suspected me and that there was nothing I could do to prove to him I wasn't to blame.

I didn't pay attention to anything that went

on in class that day. I felt sad and angry. And as if that weren't enough, I got the same welcome at home.

My mother said, "I heard you got smart."

"What do you mean?"

"I called the school and the teacher told me you put the keys on his desk this morning. Why did you take them in the first place? What makes you do things like that?"

When my father came home and the same scene repeated itself, I felt crushed.

For a long time after this I didn't study. I lost all desire to learn. I was bitter and depressed. I felt that a great injustice had been done me. At first, I tried to argue, but it didn't take me long to realize that no one believed me. All the facts were against me. I had touched the keys that were later stolen, plus they were returned in exactly the same way the teacher had suggested to my parents that they be returned. Go prove that it was all just a string of coincidences.

Slowly but surely I got back to my usual self. I finished the year with reasonable grades and said goodbye to Rabbi Cohen, feeling a lot of anger towards him. I marked that year as the worst school year ever.

I graduated and entered Rabbi Weiss's seventh grade class.

A year passed since the incident with the

keys, and then something happened that solved the mystery.

I was sitting on a bench in the school yard with Itamar, one of the kids in my class. We were watching a game of dodge-ball when suddenly Itamar asked me, "What time is it?"

I looked at where my watch should have been but my wrist was empty. It wasn't there. I couldn't believe it.

I started to look for it. I saw that Itamar was waiting for an answer, so I said to him, "I can't find my watch. It's really weird. Just a minute ago I looked at it to see how much time there was left to the break. It doesn't make sense." Itamar helped me look, but the watch had disappeared as if the ground had swallowed it up.

The bell's ring cut our search short. Recess was over. I went back to the classroom. There I renewed my search but didn't find anything.

The class (it was the last one) finally ended. I went to make a last search of the school yard and when I didn't find the watch, I decided to write a lost-and-found *hashavas aveidah* notice and hang it on the bulletin board the next day.

I walked sadly to the gate, thinking about my expensive watch that I would probably never see again.

At the gate, I met Itamar again. I told him how upset I was. I told him I wouldn't be able to sleep at night and that I didn't know what I'd tell my parents. We walked a few blocks together until we came to the corner where our paths parted.

I said goodbye to him, took a few steps towards my house, when suddenly I heard a voice cry, "Yochanan!"

I turned around to look behind me.

It was Itamar. He motioned me to wait and then walked toward me until he was standing right in front of me.

"If you want to know the truth, I was going to keep you in suspense until tomorrow. But I saw you were really upset about it, so I decided to end my game now."

Before I understood what he was talking about, he stuck his hand in his pocket and took out — my watch! Was I happy.

"Great! I can't believe it. Where did you find it?"

"I didn't find it," said Itamar.

"What do you mean?"

"I slipped it off your wrist when we were sitting next to each other."

"How could that be?" I said as I started replaying the time we had spent sitting there together. I couldn't figure out how he had managed to slip the watch off my wrist without me feeling it.

"How did you do it?" I asked with a grin.

"I'm fast with my hands," he said. "I can do a lot of things without anyone noticing."

"And it's not stealing?" I said.

"*Chas v'shalom*," he said. "I never steal. I always give back whatever I take. Usually I keep the person in suspense for a while before I return whatever I took from him. But with you, I felt so sorry for you that I gave the watch back right away."

"You should really check that out. I don't think you're allowed to do something like that," I said. "Taking something that doesn't belong to you is stealing, even if you return it."

"Okay, okay — so I won't do it again," he said. I saw he wasn't very happy about me telling him he had done something wrong.

I felt uncomfortable, so I decided to give him a compliment. "But I want you to know that I'm amazed at your dexterity. You could put on a performance for the class. It's really incredible."

I watched him glow from the compliment.

"On the other hand, maybe you shouldn't give a demonstration like that because then all the kids will guard their things and you won't be able to play any tricks."

"Are you kidding?" he said. "I practice so much that nothing will help. Let me tell you a story. A while ago I took a key chain from a kid right after he heard it jangling. It only took a couple of tries until I managed to slip the keys away from him without him even noticing."

Something clicked. "A key chain, you said?"

"Yeah. What's the problem?"

"When was this?"

"You think I remember? It was about a year ago, I guess. I don't remember exactly when."

"Whose keys were they?" I asked.

"I think they were Rabbi Cohen's. He gave them to some kid and I slipped them off him."

"Did you give them back?"

"Sure I gave them back — the same day even. After everyone went home, I went back into the classroom and put the keys on the teacher's desk. Hey, what's happening to you? How come your face turned white all of a sudden?"

"I-I'm in shock," I mumbled. "I don't believe it. You don't know how much trouble you got me into and how much I suffered because of what you did."

Now it was his turn to be shocked. "What are you talking about? What's it got to do with you?"

"You don't know what it has to do with me?"

"No. How should I?"

"You didn't see Rabbi Cohen look in my briefcase?"

"No. When did he do that?"

"Right after school."

"I wasn't in the classroom — I ran outside to

the playground. I only came in later."

"Then let me tell you what happened to me," I said. I told him the whole story from beginning to end — about the suspicion, the shame, my parents, the "proof" in finding the keys on the teacher's table, and the terrible feeling I'd had ever since then of being wrongly suspected.

Itamar looked shocked. "Everything you're telling me is news to me. I didn't know a thing about it. I only wanted to have a little fun. I didn't know the harm I caused you. Believe me, I'm really sorry. I really didn't mean it."

I believed him. My feelings went in two directions. On the one hand, I was happy to have the truth come out, even if only I knew about it. On the other hand, I was hurt and even angry with the teacher who wrongly suspected me.

"He suspected me for nothing," I said to Itamar. "I'll never forgive him for suspecting me like that and hurting me so much."

"Forget it," said Itamar. "He's not to blame. Try to understand him. If you were the teacher, wouldn't you have thought the same thing if a kid in your class jangled the key chain?"

"Easy for you to talk. You don't know what it's like to be wrongly suspected of doing something you didn't even do."

"Well, it may surprise you to hear it, but I know *exactly* what it's like," said Itamar. "And not only were my feelings hurt, but my body felt it too. They hit me for nothing."

I looked at him in astonishment. "Go ahead — tell me what happened."

"It also happened about a year ago. I walked out of our *cheder* and as usual, crossed through the Sha'arei Nachum school yard on my way home. All of a sudden, a man came out of the school, ran in my direction, and before I could say anything, dragged me into the school building.

"I thought he was a kidnapper or something, so I started screaming and putting up a fight. But then I saw the principal of the school and a few teachers coming over. They helped the man, who turned out to be the janitor, drag me into the office.

"Inside, there was a boy sitting and crying. He had a big cut on his head. Before I even knew what was happening, they started shouting at me. 'Look what you did! How dare you throw a rock at someone! Is that how a religious boy is supposed to behave? Aren't you ashamed of yourself? You'll pay for this!'

"Naturally, I denied everything. 'It wasn't me,' I said. 'It must've been someone else.'

" 'Don't lie. I saw you!' I heard the boy say.

" 'You saw me?'

" 'I sure did. You were hiding behind the building when you threw the rock. Then you

started walking home as if nothing happened, like you were totally innocent.'

"To make a long story short, all my denials didn't help a bit. One of the teachers even spanked me until the principal told him to stop. Then they called my parents to come and get me. My father came and when he saw the huge cut the boy had and the angry looks on the teachers' faces, he got the picture. He asked me, 'Why did you do it?'

"I didn't even try to argue because I knew there was no point to it. I knew he believed them, because he knows his 'precious' son. Then my father apologized to them and said that he would give me the punishment I deserved. He punished me, all right, and even now it's hard for me to forget what happened — but not just because I was punished. That happens a lot. What hurt me was that it was for no good reason. They just suspected me for something I didn't even do.

"And if you think that's the end of it, you're wrong," Itamar continued. "The next day the principal of Sha'arei Nachum came to our school's office and told our principal the whole story. The principal called Rabbi Cohen, and he yelled at me and gave me a punishment. All my protests didn't help. Naturally, they believed the principal of the other school. So all in all, I got it from the janitor and teachers at Sha'arei

Nachum, from my father, from our principal and from Rabbi Cohen. And that's for something I didn't even do. What do you have to say about that?"

Itamar's story sounded unreal to me, and soon you'll see why.

"Uh, Itamar, I'm really sorry," I heard myself begin.

"What do you have to be sorry about?" asked Itamar.

"Listen, you're telling me a story that sounds familiar. You won't believe this but...I was the one who threw that rock. I'll tell you the truth, I didn't think it would hit anyone. But after it left my hand, I saw the boy run. I could see he was hurt, so I hid behind the building. Ten minutes later, when the coast was clear, I raced home."

The two of us just sat there amazed. We both had to apologize to each other! The whole story was unbelievable.

"Look what a string of coincidences," said Itamar.

"You think it's only a string of coincidences?" I asked. "I think it's measure for measure. It's the Hand of God. We both did something and we both didn't pay for it, so it was arranged in heaven that each of us would get what was coming to him — with the added hurt of being suspected for something we never did."

"That's really something!" said Itamar in amazement. "That's incredible."

We didn't talk for a couple of minutes. We were both thinking.

"So what do you say? Should we leave it like that?" asked Itamar.

"We'll exchange apologies and end the whole thing quietly, huh?" I chuckled.

"I don't think it's a good idea to bring it up again," said Itamar, "because then we'll get punished again. You for the rock and me for the keys. Let's keep quiet and forget about it."

I thought a little before answering. "I don't think that's such a good idea."

"Why not?" asked Itamar.

"Because then we'll be doing another wrong together. We'll be making everyone wrongly suspect the innocent, which is a sin.

"Well, we're not exactly innocent," Itamar said pointedly.

We both grinned.

"Anyway, I think we have to tell everything to Rabbi Cohen and our parents," I said. "It's important to me that they know the truth. I don't want them to go on thinking that we lied."

"What will happen if they decide to punish us for what we did do?"

Again, I thought before answering. "When you get punished for what you deserve to get punished for, it hurts less. I've gotten punished lots of times, but it never hurt me as much as the time they wrongly suspected me. I think we should go to Rabbi Cohen together and tell him."

We decided to do it the next day.

After school, we asked Rabbi Cohen if we could talk to him. He agreed, and took us to the teachers' room. There we told him the real story. Rabbi Cohen remembered the two incidents and was shocked to hear the surprising twist. He looked really surprised. He sat there for a long time, asking for all the details so that he could understand how the mistake had happened. Finally he said, "If that's so, then I am guilty of wrongly suspecting an innocent person twice in one month."

We didn't say a thing. Rabbi Cohen turned to me and said, "You probably held on to a lot of anger towards me. I remember feeling that you had a grudge against me. I didn't end the year with you the same way I did with every student, did I?"

I shook my head.

The teacher sighed. "Wrongly suspecting an innocent person is a serious sin. By telling me the truth now, you're saving me from that sin and its punishment. To think that I suspected the innocent! *Innocent*," he repeated for emphasis.

The corners of my mouth began turning up

into a smile. Itamar couldn't hold himself back and burst out laughing.

"That's how children are," said the teacher. "They are very sensitive when an injustice is done to them but forget how many injustices they do to their teachers. How much trouble do children cause their teachers? Yet do teachers stop teaching? Do they start to plot revenge against the boy who did them the injustice, or try to avoid him? Why is the children's sense of justice keen only when an injustice is done them but not when they're the ones who act unfairly?"

We remained silent. I knew there was truth to what he was saying. I had used the injustice he did to me as an excuse not to study and not to listen to him.

"In any case," the teacher continued, voicing his innermost thoughts, "in any case, there is justice to that, as well. A teacher has to be much more careful than a child. He is much older and has to weigh his deeds more carefully, especially when it comes to harming the child's natural sense of fairness."

"Rabbi Cohen, you're not to blame," said Itamar. "No one in the world could have known the truth about what happened."

"That's true," said Rabbi Cohen, "but we are all commanded to judge our fellow man favorably. That means that we must judge each person favorably — even if it seems obvious that he is guilty."

"Even if it's 100 percent?"

"Even if it's 200 percent!" said the teacher. "If you had time, I would tell you something amazing."

We looked at the clock. It was 2:00. In another hour, afternoon session would start.

"I won't have time to go home for lunch," I said.

"I have an idea," said Rabbi Cohen. "Do you know my father's delicatessen?"

Of course we knew it. We used to buy salads and kugels and sometimes chopped liver every Friday afternoon at Cohen's Delicatessen. "Old Mr. Cohen," Rabbi Cohen's father, prepared all the foods himself. We felt honored to be invited there for lunch.

"Let's go. I hope I'll be able to persuade my father to tell us the story he once told me about the Ktav Sofer."

"What's that got to do with anything?" asked Itamar.

"Come and see."

We went with him, not knowing that "old Mr. Cohen" would tell us one of the most fascinating stories we'd ever heard.

The name of the story is "Who Stole the Coin?"

Who Stole the Coin?

Mr. Cohen's Story

Who Stole the Coin?

We called home to say that we wouldn't be coming for lunch, and then walked to the delicatessen, which was on the corner. Rabbi Cohen went right inside but we waited by the door. He went over to his father and whispered something in his ear. His father glanced at his watch and said something that looked like, "I don't have the time." Rabbi Cohen whispered into his ear some more and finally he turned, looked at us, and nodded.

"Good," he said. "Sit here," he pointed to an empty table.

We sat down.

He brought us soup and after that a piece of meat with a slice of his famous kugel next to it.

We ate hungrily, and when we finished, we looked up at him expectantly. He didn't disappoint us. This is the story he told us there in the delicatessen:

It all happened about a hundred and thirty years ago. About one hundred distinguished rabbis from all over Europe came to a conference to discuss important issues of the times as well as various points of halacha. The host of the gathering was none other than Rabbi Avraham Shemuel Sofer, best known as the Ktav Sofer.

The conference took place as scheduled and brought great satisfaction to the participants.

On the last day, the one hundred rabbis sat together for a farewell banquet. Speeches were heard, and halachic points was debated around the huge table. Suddenly a hush fell over the guests as the Ktav Sofer stood up. His look told them that he was about to say something of special interest.

"Before we take leave of each other," the Ktav Sofer said so all could hear, "I wish to show those present an exceptionally rare gold coin from the Second Temple period."

Whispers rippled through the hall as the Ktav Sofer held up the coin.

"This is a half-shekel coin and, to the best of my knowledge, it is the only one in the world. It is as priceless as it is rare."

Several of the rabbis stood up and went over

to see the half-shekel coin with their own eyes. They touched it, felt it, and soon the coin was being passed from hand to hand around the table. The Ktav Sofer sat down in his place at the head of the table beaming with pleasure at seeing his guests' interest in the coin.

After several minutes, the excitement subsided. The rabbis completed their meal and prepared to say *birkas hamazon*. It was then that the Ktav Sofer remembered the coin and, turning to the person sitting next to him, said, "Have they finished looking at it yet?"

The rabbi sitting next to him shrugged his shoulders and turned to ask the person sitting on the other side of him. He, too, did not know where the coin was. Finally, one of the Rabbi's assistants made an announcement. He said that the coin still hadn't been returned, and asked that now, with the meal about to end, that it please be returned.

No one made a move.

The assistants, sure that not everyone had heard the announcement, called for quiet in the hall and repeated the request.

Still, no one moved.

The rabbis looked at each other, then at the Ktav Sofer. They realized that something was terribly wrong.

The Ktav Sofer turned pale. He stood up and

asked, "Please — the coin has still not been returned to me. Perhaps it fell on one of the tables?"

A search of the tables and the floor underneath was made, yet the coin was still not found.

Confusion reigned. All those present realized that the coin couldn't have just disappeared. Someone must have taken it...and kept it.

The elder rabbis began feverish consultations about what to do. Something like this had never happened before, that a coin disappeared during such a distinguished rabbinical conference...and not because it was lost. What would people say?

If the coin had been worth only a small sum, or even if it had been worth thousands of zlotys, the matter would have been kept quiet. But the value of the coin was priceless.

"*Rabbosai*," the Ktav Sofer called out to those assembled, "I beg of you! This is a very unfortunate occurrence. The coin you all saw is the only one in existence. I beg of you to find it, for if not, I will have no choice but to give instructions that each person here search the clothes of another."

They all sat there open-mouthed. The matter was fast becoming quite serious. What a desecration of God's Name there would be were it to become known that at the conference of the most esteemed rabbis in Europe a valuable coin was stolen, and that all the rabbis were searched!

Several long minutes passed. The hall rocked with the sounds of the rabbis talking, yet the coin was not returned to its owner.

"There is no choice then," announced the Ktav Sofer. "I command each person present to search the clothes of his fellow so that the good name of all the Torah leaders of Europe will not be besmirched."

The rabbis prepared to begin their humiliating task, when just then, from the back of the hall, came the voice of an elderly rabbi who served as the leader of a small community in Hungary.

"Begging your pardon," he said softly, "but it is not seemly to conduct such a search. Please, make another search of the hall. Perhaps the coin fell and rolled under the table?"

The elderly rabbi's voice trembled with emotion. Everyone looked at him, but he said no more, and waited patiently for the Ktav Sofer to speak.

"Let it be as our venerable guest suggests," said the Ktav Sofer. "Search the hall."

Thus the distinguished rabbis of Europe found themselves bending down under the table, lifting up the corners of the rug, searching every inch of the floor, even sifting through the food remnants to check and see if perhaps the coin had rolled there.

But nothing was found.

"If so," announced the Ktav Sofer, "all options have been exhausted. We must proceed with the search."

The rabbis again began their preparations for the search, deciding who would search whom, when suddenly, everyone saw the elderly rabbi stand up on a chair and cry out, "Please do not do this! It is a desecration of God's Name. Perhaps you can try looking again? Perhaps...?"

By now, the patience of those present was fast reaching its end. "We have searched more than enough. The time has come to conclude the matter, despite the unpleasantness involved."

There were those who eyed the elderly rabbi suspiciously. It was safe to assume that the only person who was against the search was the very person who had stolen the coin.

Suddenly the elderly rabbi said, "I will tell you why I am against the search." He took a deep breath. "It is because I myself brought a similar coin to this gathering and I know you will suspect that this is the coin lost by our esteemed rabbi and teacher." Then, to the astonishment of all, he took out of his pocket a coin identical to the one missing.

There it was — the missing coin — in the

hand of one of their fellow rabbis!

"It was in his pocket," they murmured.

Everyone looked at the coin and at the rabbi in deep shock. Until then, the Hungarian rabbi had been known as a true *tzaddik* and an important halachic authority. Everyone sighed over the fact that in his old age, the elderly sage's behavior was casting a shadow over his whole life.

The elderly rabbi, who apparently realized that those present were looking at him in disbelief, repeated, "This is not the coin that disappeared. This coin belongs to me."

Everyone stood there staring at the rabbi, not knowing what to think. There were those who judged him favorably, assuming that he had done something foolish in his old age.

But most of those present treated the new claim with scorn and derision. Well they knew that the coin in question was the rare half-shekel coin from the Second Temple era, of which there was only one in existence. In any case, the rabbi's guilt was as plain as the writing on the wall.

As they were standing there in confusion, upset and angry, a youth of about fifteen, a cook's assistant, quickly made his way from the kitchen to the center of the hall. He went straight to the Ktav Sofer and said, "I found the coin!"

One hundred pairs of eyes stared at him. He

threw the coin up in the air and everyone saw that it was exactly like the one held by the elderly Hungarian rabbi!

It's hard to describe the shock that hit everyone. They all felt their knees tremble. They realized that a terrible thing had happened there in the hall, something that had practically no explanation.

In the silence, it was easy to hear the youth speaking. "I searched through the garbage and found the coin amongst the scraps of meat."

The Ktav Sofer told everyone to sit down again in their places. He asked the youth to sit on his left. The youth declined, out of respect, and remained standing. The Ktav Sofer then turned to the elderly rabbi and asked him to sit on his right. To the rabbis assembled around the table he declared, "It seems clear to me that God has presented us with this terrible situation so that we can learn a great deal more than what we learned all the days of the conference. Please, my distinguished guest, tell us your story."

The elderly rabbi, whose eyes were filled with tears of relief, spoke with difficulty. "I came here from the town where I live with a rare coin in my pocket, which I had planned on showing you, my dear friends and colleagues, right at the closing moments, as is our custom.

"When our esteemed leader Rabbi Avraham

Shemuel Sofer stood and held up a similar coin, I was naturally quite surprised and slightly disappointed at seeing that the coin in my hand was not the only one in the world. I listened as our great rabbi and teacher said that his was the only coin in existence and decided not to tell anyone about my coin so as not to contradict his words and embarrass him in front of everyone.

"Then, when they announced that the coin was missing, and the decision was made to search all the rabbis, I realized the magnitude of my predicament. I knew that once the coin was found in my pocket, not a single person here would judge me favorably and believe what I said, that the coin belonged to me. I knew that I would look like both a thief and a liar. Therefore, I opposed the search, hoping that in the meantime the coin would be found.

"This was not to be, and so I endured some of the most terrible moments of my life, when I was suspected wrongly. I am certain that the great humiliation and terrible shame that were my lot atoned for all my sins. Thus it is easy for me to forgive with a full heart anyone who mistakenly suspected me and did not judge me favorably."

All those present felt moved by the elderly rabbi's heartfelt words. He continued, "However, it is my wish that what you witnessed today remain forever engraved in your hearts and that

you pass it on to your communities and to the members of your families. We are commanded to judge each person favorably — not only when there is good reason to do so. Even at those times when a person's guilt seems one hundred percent certain, try to extend yourselves to find a point of merit, and may my example bear witness like one hundred witnesses."

Then the elderly rabbi said, "I ask of you only this: Imagine my feelings if this wonderful youth had not found the coin. Would a single one of you have believed me? Would anyone in my community have believed me? Would anyone in my family have believed me? Imagine the shame and humiliation I would have felt until the day of my death."

All eyes filled with tears. The guests thought about the terrible sin that might have accompanied them till their deaths — the sin of suspecting the innocent — and shuddered.

Then they all remembered the youth who had saved them from that sin.

"What make you search through the refuse?" the Ktav Sofer asked him.

The hall fell silent, waiting to hear his answer. The boy was embarrassed at first, but after a slight hesitation, his thin voice could be heard: "The truth is, I saw all the rabbis looking at this rabbi...and I saw that everyone was so positive about it...but I thought to myself that it couldn't be that a rabbi would steal the coin! That's exactly what I said to myself: It couldn't be that a rabbi stole it! I believed the rabbi who said the coin belonged to him...because that's what he said...and it couldn't be that he would lie. So I decided that even if no one else believed him, I would. I went to the big garbage pail, I dumped everything on the ground, and I started to go through it by hand until I found the coin, and then I ran to the rabbi... Wait a minute — why is everyone crying? Honored Rabbi, did I do something wrong?"

All the rabbis sobbed at the simplicity of the youth and his innocent faith. Several of them buried their heads in their hands, embarrassed to look their colleagues in the eye.

"Do you know why we're crying?" said the Ktav Sofer to the guileless youth. "It is because your sincere words are a rebuke to us all, for we did not think as you did. Our Sages tell us: 'From all my students I have grown wise' yet I never imagined," said the Ktav Sofer, "that a youth of fifteen would teach us more than anyone else. What is your name?" he asked.

"Meir Zvi Cohen," said the youth.

"Now listen to what I am going to say," the Ktav Sofer said to the boy. "I owe you a tremendous debt of gratitude. You not only saved me and all these great rabbis from the grievous sin of suspecting the innocent but you have also taught us a lofty level of judging everyone favorably. I want to repay you. Thus I will bless you in front of everyone here that in the merit of your saving us, you and your descendants will be saved from every trouble and misfortune, and that Satan will have no power over you, and that you and your descendants will merit long life and will never, ever lack for anything."

The Ktav Sofer rose from his place and warmly embraced the youth. That's when he smelled the odor that clung to the youth from his search through the garbage. Yet the Ktav Sofer was not repelled by the smell nor by the dirt and continued to hug the youth. As he did so, he murmured a cryptic sentence in the boy's ear: "The refuse will wash off but it will always be ready to come and save you from trouble."

Few heard those last words. The conference drew to a close and the attendees dispersed, filled with emotion, to their various communities.

As the elderly Mr. Cohen concluded his story we were left sitting around the table amazed at the remarkable tale. Somehow, though, we had the feeling that the story wasn't over.

Mr. Cohen took a deep breath and continued. "That youth grew up and went through World

War I. He married and established a large
family, with grandchildren and great-grand-
children, and then came the Second World War.
The family was scattered, sent to various work
camps. The youth in the story was by then an old
man of 95 and I could stay here talking for
another two hours telling you what he went
through to survive. I'll only tell you that he hid in
the last ghetto along with five other elderly Jews.
The Germans killed everyone except him. He was
saved through very strange circumstances.

"There was a German truck full of garbage.
He jumped into it and buried himself under the
garbage. The German driver drove the truck to a
garbage dump in a desolate place, far from
human habitation. From that moment on, until
the end of the war, the old man survived on
scraps of garbage that were thrown onto the
dump. You can't imagine what a time that was.
The truth is, he didn't even know about the war's
end. He only found out about it months
afterwards when he overheard a conversation
between two garbage truck drivers.

"After the war, he made aliyah. To his great
surprise, he discovered that his entire family,
including all his children and grandchildren, had
also survived and made aliyah. Meir Zvi Cohen
died forty years ago at the age of 100. He merited
long life, as did his descendants."

"Where did he live?" I asked.

"Here, upstairs, in this building where the delicatessen is. Now his little boy, who is ninety years old, lives here. That's me." And then he added, "Is there a problem? Why are there tears in your eyes?"

"Old Mr. Cohen," we murmured. We had never dreamed of a story like this.

"Old Mr. Cohen," Mr. Cohen repeated after us. "*Baruch Hashem*, so far the Ktav Sofer's blessing has been fulfilled and I hope that it will continue to be fulfilled in my beloved son, Meir Zvi, your teacher (who was named after my father, may he rest in peace), who brings me so much *nachas* and honor."

It was exactly 3:00 o'clock. We said the after-blessing, thanked Mr. Cohen for his fascinating story, and raced back to school with Rabbi Cohen. (Rabbi Cohen taught in the afternoons, too.) On the way, he said to us, "I know the story, yet every time I hear it I feel moved. I've decided what I'm going to do about what happened. It's very important to me that I continue my grandfather's tradition of judging everyone favorably, so I want to correct my mistake."

We told him that we forgave him with all our hearts. Besides, we both really did deserve a punishment. True, not for what we were suspected of. But the main thing was that we had gotten what we really deserved.

Still, Rabbi Cohen insisted, saying that he wasn't satisfied with leaving it at that. He had suspected us wrongly and now he had to fix things. He refused to say how.

In the first class, he came into the room and asked the afternoon teacher for a few minutes so that he could say something to the class. He quietly stated in front of everyone that the previous year he had suspected me of taking some keys and Itamar of throwing a rock, but that now it had come to light that this wasn't true. He didn't saying anything about what we really did (that I threw the rock and Itamar took the keys), and so he turned us into *tzaddikim gemurim*, completely righteous, even though we were far from that. That night he called our parents and told them the same thing. He didn't tell them the other part. We did that ourselves.

Ever since, whenever I pass Cohen's Delicatessen, I think of the story and remind myself about my promise to always judge my friends and everyone favorably.

Memory Game

Eli's Story

Memory Game

At the beginning of the year, our sixth grade secular studies teacher came into the classroom holding a huge bag full of different things.

He asked us to put all the desks together in the center of the room to make one big desk and then to sit around it. Then he dumped out the contents of the bag and spread it around on the huge table we had made.

"I'm going to give you a memory exercise," he said. "You have ten minutes to look at all the things here on the table. At the end of the ten minutes, I'm going to gather them all up and give you each a piece of paper on which you are to write down everything you saw. Whoever remembers the most things is the winner."

This sounded really interesting. We started to look at the stuff spread out on the table.

There was an umbrella, an apricot pit, various sized marbles, a folded piece of paper, a broken Walkman, headphones for the Walkman, a shoe box, one shoe, a screw, a nail, a piece of Lego, a candy wrapper, a hanger, a ball, a balloon, a straw, a diskette, a toy car — and that's only a small part of what was there. There were dozens and dozens of things.

Everyone stared at the pile, concentrating hard, trying to remember everything. So did I. The ten minutes went by fast.

Then the teacher collected all the things and gave out an order: "Write!"

When I started to write, it didn't take me long to find out that I could hardly remember most of what was on the table. I quickly wrote down the most obvious things. The rest I had to drag out of my memory. It was very hard. At the end of ten minutes, the teacher collected the papers.

I managed to remember 33 things.

There were some kids in the class who wrote down less things than I did, but most remembered more — 40, 45, with Zevi getting the most with 58 things. My friend Shloimi only managed to write down 25 things, and you'll soon find out why I'm telling you all this.

Then the teacher said, "Do you know how many items there were? 120!"

That means the best one of us remembered

less than half the things. The teacher wrote down the results, and the class was over.

After two weeks, we asked him if we could play the memory game again. This time I went up to 42 items and the rest of my classmates also got more.

Shloimi was able to remember 30.

We started to like the game, and our teacher, seeing that, made playing it conditional on our good behavior and an increase in the class's grade point average. When he was satisfied with us, he played the game with us (each time with different things).

From game to game we would talk about how much fun it was. We came to the conclusion that it showed how much memory each of us had. We made up a list. Zevi came out in first place, I was eighth, and Shloimi was 22nd out of the 30 boys in our class.

When the teacher heard about it, he told us that our list wasn't right at all. "Even the boy who is last could be first if he wanted to," he said.

"We all want to be first!" we cried out. "We just don't remember well."

"That's because you don't use your memories enough," he said.

Everything I'm telling you took place from Elul to around Kislev. On *Rosh Chodesh* Teves, we played the game again. Shloimi shot up from being number 22 to number 11. The kids in class hardly noticed. There were a few kids who whistled in appreciation, but usually you only look at the top 10.

Two weeks after that, we played the game again. Shloimi moved up to fifth place.

On *Rosh Chodesh* Adar, he got to first place. He managed to guess 100 items out of 120.

The class was amazed. We were all sure he had some kind of a trick. He assured us that he didn't have any trick — he just remembered all the things. Since we couldn't prove any different, we kept quiet.

On *Rosh Chodesh* Nisan, pandemonium broke out.

Shloimi was able to remember 115 out of the 120 items.

The whole class claimed he must be doing something not quite kosher. "It can't be that a kid who was so far down can suddenly remember so much."

The teacher stepped in. "It does look pretty strange. Even I wouldn't be able to remember everything."

A hush fell on the classroom. Everyone looked at Shloimi suspiciously. Suddenly Simcha said, "I have an idea. Let's make a test for Shloimi. We'll all go out and collect things and after school we'll see if he really remembers or if it's just a trick."

We all looked at Shloimi, but he stayed calm. "Okay by me," was all he said.

The game was set for the following day. All the kids in class gathered different items and came equipped with all sorts of things. Out of everything brought, we chose 120 items.

After school, we put the tables next to each other and spread out the items. After ten minutes of observation, we passed out pieces of paper to everyone and sat down to write.

When we finished writing, it turned out that we had all gone up in the number of items we remembered (because each of us had himself collected a few things, and also because we were more accustomed to the game). Zevi was able to remember more than 90 things, but what shocked us more than anything was that Shloimi managed to remember all 120 items.

We didn't know what to say. We were positive there had to be a solution to the riddle, but we didn't know what it was. One thing was for sure: Shloimi couldn't have known the list of items beforehand. Even we, who did know all of them, hadn't managed to top him.

We asked him to tell us the secret. At first he said, "I just remember and that's all!" But when we pressed him further, he said, "I'd tell you, but I'm scared."

"Scared?" we asked. "Of what?"

"If you want me to tell, I'll have to let you in on a secret that only I and one other person know about, and this secret is going to make a few kids in the class angry."

This was starting to sound mysterious. "We promise we won't get angry," we all said in unison.

"I want everyone to sign a piece of paper saying he won't get angry at me. You too, Eli — you have to sign it too, okay?"

"Me? What does it have to do with me?"

"You'll see. It just does," said Shloimi.

I started trying to think of what the secret could be. My curiosity grew from minute to minute. I agreed to sign anything he wanted as long as he'd tell us his secret and explain how it was connected to me.

The rest of the kids in the class were just as curious as I was and quickly signed the note in which we wrote that we promised not to get mad at Shloimi. He took the note, read it, and then said, "Okay. Today I'll write the whole story, and tomorrow I'll let you read it."

Actually, we wanted him to tell us right away, but he insisted that he wanted to write it down because he was too embarrassed to tell it to our faces. That meant that what he was going to tell us would hurt our feelings a little. I wonder what it could be? I thought to myself. And what does it have to do with the memory game?

The story came the next day, photocopied several times. We read it avidly. It really was connected to me, and also to a few other kids. The story did make us feel embarrassed, but it sure didn't make us mad at Shloimi. Not at all. Instead, it made us appreciate him a lot and even feel very grateful to him.

It sounds like he wrote a riddle, doesn't it?

That's why you'd better read Shloimi's story yourself. You'll be amazed. It has nothing to do with the memory game, but with a few things that happened recently that really do involve me, I'm ashamed to say, and six other boys in the class. So just turn the page and read Shloimi's story.

Angels in the Night

Shloimi's Story

Angels in the Night

My story is going to shock several of my best friends here in Bnei Brak, but I decided the time has come to tell it to everyone, because there's a lot to learn from it.

In my neighborhood there's a workshop that repairs bicycles. I'm sure you know what that kind of a place looks like: messy, full of wheels, handlebars, chains, various sized tires, inner tubes, screws, metal rods and gears of all sorts and types.

And, of course, there are dozens of bicycles, some new, and some old ones that look unusable. The owner uses these for spare parts.

The workshop is located at the bottom of a dark, damp stairwell. It's open a few hours in the afternoon. That's when it turns into a place bustling with life. Lots of kids go there to fix a flat tire, change a bent or broken chain, buy a bell, or fix a pedal.

The workshop is also a meeting place for all the kids in the neighborhood, who hang around there for hours until Mr. Katz, the owner, goes home. It's not exactly a real store. The basement workshop is located in an abandoned building that must belong to Mr. Katz.

Mr. Katz is an elderly man of, maybe, seventy. They say he's been fixing carriages and bicycles since he was ten. My father told me that when he was younger, most of Mr. Katz's work was fixing carriages because "Who had bicycles then?"

Mr. Katz always worked quickly and quietly. He spoke only when someone blocked his light or talked loudly and disturbed his concentration. And since tons of kids were always bunched up by the entrance, talking loudly and crowding around him, two things usually happened: his light was blocked and his concentration was disturbed. That meant that Mr. Katz wound up shouting at the kids most of the time, asking them to move away and be quiet.

It would help for about five minutes. Then they'd be back, crowding around him and talking.

The story I'm going to tell you started about two months ago. A bunch of us from my school were hanging around in Mr. Katz's workshop. It was pretty noisy. We talked, shouted at the top of our lungs, and most of all, crowded around Mr. Katz, who was busy repairing a fancy ten-speed bike. Mr. Katz shouted at us a few times, as usual. We'd be quiet for a few minutes, but then we'd forget again.

Suddenly Mr. Katz stood up and declared, "I've had it with you guys. Get out of the office!" (That's what he called his workshop, an "office," even though it was about as organized as a...as a goat pen).

This was a new one for us. He had never chased us or any other kids out of his store. We must have crossed a red line.

He ushered us out of the room and slammed the iron door shut. We were left standing outside, angry and humiliated.

"Who does he think he is to chase us away like that?" said Moishe.

"We're giving him business and that's how he repays us?" I said.

"We can't let him get away with it," said Eli.

We started banging on the gate to the building. Mr. Katz didn't open. We banged louder. Suddenly he came out and ran after us, waving his arms. Naturally we made a quick escape on our bikes.

It dawned on us that he wasn't going to fix our bikes that day.

Night fell. The light still burned in Mr. Katz's

shop. We watched from afar, still feeling hurt and angry at being chased away like that.

All of a sudden, we saw him leave the building, shut the light, and walk away.

We stayed where we were.

A few minutes later, we walked over to the stairwell and looked at the crowded workshop, at all the bicycles that were tied to each other with one long, heavy chain.

It was Eli who came up with the idea of playing a prank.

"Let's make 'Purim' in his office," he said, going over to the pile of bikes. He pulled off a chain that was attached to the handlebars of one bike and switched it with a different chain that was hanging on a different bike waiting to be repaired. He started to mix up everything in the workshop, and switched the places of all the wheels that were standing up alongside different bikes. We stood and watched, not understanding exactly what he was doing. After a few minutes, he finished and came over to us.

"Don't you get it?" he said. "Tomorrow he'll have double the work. He'll have to find the right part for each bike. Instead of fixing bicycles, he'll have to put together the piece of a puzzle. Maybe that way he'll learn his lesson."

We burst out laughing. "That's a great idea," we said, imagining how the scene would look.

After a quarter of an hour of talk and laughter, we split up to go home, promising ourselves we'd go back the next day to watch Mr. Katz put together the puzzle we set up for him.

I went home. I took a shower and got ready for bed, thinking, naturally, about what had just happened. I pictured Mr. Katz coming to his workshop the next day and immediately realized that it wasn't just a prank, but a mean trick. I reminded myself that he wasn't some enemy who had done us evil, but an elderly man of seventy who repaired our bikes. We were the ones who had bothered him. True, he had chased us away. But that was because we had gone too far. And besides, maybe he hadn't been feeling well and that's why he had to send us away.

That thought made me really regret what had been done. *That's what you are?* an inner voice said to me. *A mean kid who bothers other people?*

I wondered how I could right this wrong before it was too late. Then suddenly I had a brainstorm.

I got dressed and told my mother I wanted to go out for a few minutes to fix something on my bike. My mother looked at her watch. It was 9:00 p.m. and my request seemed strange, but because I often have requests like that, she agreed.

I left the house and ran towards the stairwell of the abandoned building.

Everything was dark. A frightening silence hung over the place. The only sound you could hear was the sound of my breathing. I made my way to the workshop. Dim light penetrated from the street lamp so that after a minute my eyes adjusted and I was able to see what was going on.

The first thing I did was return the bigger chain to the ten-speed bike and put the smaller chain back next to the green bike that it belonged to. I put the small wheel next to the bike with the training wheels, and the large pedal alongside the mountain bike. After that I tried to remember the other swaps Eli had made, and I remembered to put the tools back in their places. Then I decided that if I tried any more to put things in place I'd only make things worse, so all I did was fix my share of the mess. Then I left and went home as fast as I could, sweating from the tension and effort.

From the way my mother looked at me, I realized I was in trouble.

"Take a look at yourself," she said. "You're full of black oil stains. What happened? Did the chain fall off your bicycle?"

I gave her an apologetic look and went to shower again. I fell asleep fast, this time with a really good feeling. I felt I had done a good deed.

The next day, we got to class. I didn't say anything about it to my friends, of course. I pretended to be just as excited as they were about going to see Mr. Katz's "office" later. Actually, I really was excited — but for reasons entirely different from theirs.

That afternoon we went to the workshop. Mr. Katz seemed especially irritable. He was constantly looking for things and got very angry when he couldn't find them. Our voices bothered him even more than they had the day before and he told us, "Excuse me, but I have a big mess here and I can't serve anyone because my time is taken up today with nonsense."

Out of all the kids gathered there, only three knew what he was talking about. I was glad I had fixed most of the damage in time.

When I went outside, I saw that Eli had shared the secret with Simcha. Simcha looked really excited about the new prank. And then I caught on that what happened yesterday was about to repeat itself.

That night, the four of us went into the stairwell. This time I decided to use my brain to remember from where everything was taken and where it was put. I couldn't write it down because then they'd suspect me. I just wrote it down in my mind.

I myself worked slowly. I changed everything twice...so that at least I didn't do any harm. They didn't notice that in the end I was taking all the things I moved and putting them back where they belonged. And they noticed even less that I was putting back all the things they moved.

After a quarter of an hour of messing things up, four kids left — three of them happy and pleased with themselves, one of them concentrating. I didn't talk to my friends because I was afraid I'd forget what I was repeating to myself.

It got dark. I said goodbye to my friends, waited a few minutes until they had gone home, and then I went back. This time I came equipped with a pocket flashlight. Within a few minutes I had returned most of the items to their places. I was especially proud of remembering where to replace several screws belonging to a bicycle hubcap. If they were missing, it would have caused Mr. Katz a big headache. There were only a few things I didn't touch and that was because I didn't know where they belonged.

When I got home, my slight delay went unnoticed but the dirt on my clothes didn't. This time my mother wasn't quiet about it.

"Tell me something, are you a baby that you have to come home with such dirty clothes? What gotten into you? Have you suddenly turned into a bicycle repairman?"

She didn't know how close she was to the truth.

I decided to enjoy the whole thing. My friends played a trick on an elderly man who never did anyone any harm and I played a good trick back on them that undid their trick.

I was happy that the number of times we visited Mr. Katz's workshop after hours became fewer, partly because playing tricks gets boring sometimes, and partly because he didn't seem irritated at all. My friends were mad as anything, though. They'd come to the workshop to watch Mr. Katz struggle with the mess and instead, all they'd see was that he had already managed to return each thing to its place. That took all the fun out of it.

Still, I had to stay on the alert because whenever Mr. Katz got irritated and yelled at them, they'd "rearrange" his things again — which meant that I had to rearrange them back.

Four months passed, until there came one special night, a night I'll never forget as long as I live.

It was after a few days when six kids led by Eli turned the workshop totally upside-down so that I had to work longer than usual at night and use my memory in a way that really gave me a headache.

One night, after they finished their job of wreaking havoc, I came back home and my mother asked me to help her clean up the house. It took about an hour, and after that I asked her, as usual, if I could go out on my bike. My mother wasn't against it but she gave me a kind of helpless look that said, "What can I do with him?" In no time at all, I was on my way to the "office."

I got there. The place was a mess. As usual, I used all my brain cells to take stock of the place, and then I started working hard and fast. I moved bicycles from place to place, I exchanged chains, screws, tools, replacement parts and wheels — and then I saw a three-speed bike that was missing a chain.

I remembered right away that one of the kids had tossed the chain in the air, throwing it up towards the ceiling. I remembered clearly how I had shouted at him, "What do you think you're doing? That could hit someone and kill him!" But he was having fun and I couldn't make him stop. The chain had flown just inches from my head and landed on top of a heavy closet.

How could I not forget it?

I went over to the closet to climb up on it. To do that, I had to move a wooden table that was leaning against the wall. It weighed a ton. I started to drag it and there, underneath it, I saw something that made my blood freeze.

Someone was sitting there, under the table, watching me.

"*Yi-i-i-i!*" I screamed.

He looked huge. In the dark you could only

see his eyes bulging from his huge face. I saw his big hands, too. They looked scary.

For several long moments I stood there frozen in place looking at him, and then he moved slightly forward. Rays of light from the street lamp hit him, and then suddenly I realized that the man in the dark was none other than Mr. Katz himself.

I was terrified. What was he doing here now?

I was paralyzed with fear. He stood up and started coming closer to me.

"It-it w-wasn't m-me...I promise. It was the other kids." I stopped. I knew there was no point in talking. He wouldn't believe me. No one would have believed me. Not even the police.

In a flash, it dawned on me how much trouble I had gotten myself into.

He stepped towards me and I flinched and started to step backwards. I took a few steps like that until I bumped into a bicycle and fell over backwards.

In one second, he was on me. I started to yell in fear, "It wasn't me! Don't do anything to me! I promise. First let me say something."

That's when I heard him say, "Take it easy, kid. Don't get so worked up. I know everything. Relax. I'm not going to do anything to you."

I looked at him in disbelief. The thought flashed through my mind that maybe he wanted

to calm me down so that I wouldn't shout for help, but the expression on his face made it obvious that he really wasn't angry. Actually, he looked the opposite of angry. Now I could see his face clearly. His eyes looked gentle. He looked at me with compassion and a certain wonderment, not anger. His face looked friendly.

I waited for him to say something. I couldn't run away anyway.

"Relax. I know it wasn't you who turned my office upside-down. I was here the whole week, when you reorganized things," he said.

I couldn't believe my ears. "You were here? Then why...why didn't you catch the ones who..."

"It's a long story," said Mr. Katz. "If you want, I'll tell it to you, but not like this, with you lying on the floor. First of all, get up, relax, take a chair, drink a glass of water, and then you'll hear everything."

I stood up. Mr. Katz went over to the corner of the room and filled a plastic cup with water from the faucet. He offered me the cup, and both of us sat down on opposite sides of the work table under which he had hidden.

"I've been working here forty years already," Mr. Katz began his story. "I know the place so well, that if someone moves things around here, I feel it.

"A few months ago, I felt there was some

strange 'movement' of the things here in the office. At first, I thought that maybe I was getting old and imagining things, but after a few days, I knew my hunch was correct.

"The first month, I didn't know what to do. I thought of lying in ambush, but I didn't have the strength to stay here after my regular work hours. About a month ago, I had several errands to run in town. I decided to leave the office and return in an hour.

"When I came back and went into the office, my heart sank. From the very first day I began work, there had never been such a mess. It took a few minutes before I could even take it all in. I began wondering how I could ever get the place back into shape again. I managed to find a chain that I knew belonged somewhere else, but more than that I didn't know. I got mixed up and I even started to think that I'd never be able to go on working in this office. More than anything, I worried about the people who had left their bicycles with me. What would I say to them? A younger man might have rolled up his sleeves and started working long and hard, but I'm an old man. I barely have enough strength for my regular work, certainly not enough to put back in order an office that's been turned upside-down.

"I sat in the dark," continued Mr. Katz, "and felt like crying. I didn't know what to do. Then suddenly I heard footsteps coming from the entrance to the building. I decided to hide under the table to see who was coming.

"I saw a boy walk in confidently and start to move things around. At first, I wanted to pounce on him, but something made me watch his movements. To my surprise, I saw that he went over and put things back in their places, moved bicycles, handlebars, wheels, and screws. In only a few minutes, as if by magic, he had returned everything to its place. The boy acted as if he knew the place well; he moved confidently, without hesitation. When he was done, he looked around the office again. That's when I recognized him as the boy who sometimes came to my office with a bunch of kids who like to pester me.

"I recognized *you!*" said Mr. Katz.

I shuddered, but didn't say a word. Mr. Katz continued his story.

"I still didn't understand exactly what was going on here, who was making a mess in the office and who was putting things back. I was very curious. I decided to lie in ambush every night. A whole week passed before you all came again. I watched you closely and saw that you didn't mess up a thing. I saw how you watched your friends' actions carefully, and then I understood everything.

"I decided to wait here even after you all left.

Sure enough, half an hour later, you came in and within ten minutes, you rearranged what it would have taken me a week to do."

Mr. Katz paused to look at me. I couldn't believe what I had just heard. Never in a million years did I dream that someone was watching me all that time.

"I went home," continued Mr. Katz, "but I couldn't fall asleep. Do you know why?"

"Why?"

"Because I was so excited about seeing a 'new Chofetz Chaim.' "

"What?!"

"Just what you heard. In my opinion, you are the Chofetz Chaim of this generation."

"What's the connection?" I asked.

"I'll tell you," said Mr. Katz.

"Rabbi Yisrael Meir HaKohen, called the Chofetz Chaim, was born and raised in the city of Radin. In those days, there were no faucets, of course, and the water was brought to the homes by a water carrier. Just like there are today, so too, back then there were children who liked to play pranks, and one day a certain boy had an idea. He took a group of children to the village well in the night. Very quietly, they turned the handle and lowered the water carrier's two buckets into the well. When they felt the buckets were full, they turned the handle together, raised the full buckets, placed them next to the well, and ran triumphantly home."

"What's the point?" I asked.

"The point is, that it was ten below zero outside. What do you think happened to the water in the buckets?"

"It froze," I said.

"Right. That means that in the morning, when the water carrier came for his buckets, he had to work for a few hours to break up the ice in them, much to the delight of the boys who peeked out at him through the windows of their homes.

"How mean," I said.

"They weren't exactly mean," explained Mr. Katz. "They were children who just didn't think. They did something mean without thinking about what they were doing.

"One day they decided to get Yisrael Meir to join them. He was with them, saw the prank they pulled, and didn't say a thing."

"Nothing?" I asked.

"Nothing. But at night, when everyone was sleeping, Yisrael Meir went out in the freezing cold, shivering all over, went to the well and poured the water out of the buckets. Then he went home quietly and went to sleep.

"The first morning, the children thought the water had spilled out accidentally. But when they saw the water carrier take his empty buckets every day, fill them, and bring water to the houses, they decided that it must be angels who poured out the water for him every night — which was true in a way. They decided that the water carrier was a hidden *tzaddik*, and they stopped bothering him.

"Now what do you say about that? Who was the angel? Who was the hidden *tzaddik*?"

"The Chofetz Chaim," I said.

"So now do you know why I called you the Chofetz Chaim of this generation?" asked Mr. Katz.

I didn't answer. I didn't know what to say. I knew that I didn't come close to the level of the Chofetz Chaim, but what had happened with me was pretty similar, so I didn't have an answer.

"This past month," continued Mr. Katz, "I stayed here every day and just waited for your friends to come and turn everything upside-down so that I could watch you put everything back again. Seeing a favorite childhood story repeat itself before my eyes gave me great pleasure and satisfaction. I could have put an end to it by catching all of you, but I didn't want to. I didn't want to miss seeing my own private 'Chofetz Chaim.' Do you know what I mean?"

Mr. Katz glanced at his watch. "It's late and they must be worried about you at home. Go home, son. You won't have to rearrange this place any more because tomorrow I will go to the parents of the other boys and ask them to take care of the matter. But I feel I owe you something. The fact that I let you work so hard bothers me. That's why I decided several days ago to compensate you. Here" — Mr. Katz walked to the corner of the room and brought out a shiny new twelve-speed bike — "this is yours," he said. "And do me a favor, don't ruin your 'Chofetz Chaim' image in my eyes. Ride it carefully, and only when there's no traffic, and try to be a Chofetz Chaim. Okay?"

"Thanks," I said. "But I want you to know that thanks to this whole thing I got a bigger present than a twelve-speed bicycle."

This time it was Mr. Katz's turn to be surprised. "Really? From whom?"

"From Hashem. Putting things back in place meant straining my memory. Thanks to the months I spent here, I remember practically everything I see. That helps me a lot in learning and also...in games," I said.

Now, when my friends read this story, I hope they won't be mad at me. I hope they'll realize that all I did was save them from the big sin of causing damage and anguish to another person.

Flat Tire

Dudi's Story

Flat Tire

What I want to tell you about happened two weeks ago when I was standing with my father at the bus stop in our neighborhood, which is on the outskirts of Bnei Brak.

All of a sudden, I heard a strange sound coming from the street. We turned to see what it was all about. At first we didn't notice anything, but then, a couple of seconds later, we saw that the noise came from the direction of a car that had just gotten a flat tire.

My father motioned to the driver to stop. The driver, who apparently also realized that his car was wobbling slightly, stopped a few yards in front of the bus stop and got out of the car to inspect the tire.

He opened the trunk and took out a jack and a tool to open the wheel's screws. He put the jack under the car and started to pump.

We watched what was happening. It didn't take long to see that whatever the driver was doing wasn't working. Every time the car lifted up slightly, it fell right back down again. The man looked miserable.

My father turned to me and said, "Let's go help him." We walked over.

"Would you like some help?" my father asked the driver.

"What took you so long?" said the driver angrily. "Now's when you remember to offer some help? I've been here half an hour already and suddenly you decide to be generous?"

I couldn't believe it. My father is a distinguished Torah scholar. That's not the way people talk to him. Besides, the driver had only been there three minutes at the most — definitely not half an hour.

I expected my father to let him know what a chutzpah it was to talk that way, but my father only said softly, "It seems to me that you haven't put the jack in the right place. There's a special indent where the jack has to go and that's the only way it'll work."

The driver looked at my father scornfully and hissed, "Another wise guy who thinks he knows cars."

The minute he said that, the car fell down

again, almost straight onto his foot. I started snickering, but my father covered my mouth with his hand and whispered, "It's forbidden to feel happy at another person's humiliation."

"Maybe you'll show me how to do it instead of standing there like a *golem?*" the man shouted at my father.

My father suffered this insult in silence too. He went over to the car, bent down, peered under it, and immediately discovered the right place. He took the jack, set it in the right place, and started pumping the handle.

The car began to lift up fast.

"Maybe you'll do me a favor and stop smoking?" the driver barked sarcastically at my father.

My father stopped pumping the jack and looked at him. "Listen," he said, "I'm willing to help you, but I'm not willing to be your dish rag. One more comment from you and I'm leaving."

The driver kept quiet and my father continued his work in silence.

He opened the screws and, with the help of the driver, removed the old wheel.

That's when our bus came.

"I have to go now," my father said. "I'm in a hurry to get to an important lecture."

"This is how you leave me?" said the driver. "That's no way to act. You'd go off and leave me

just like that, not knowing how to fix it?"

My father glanced at his watch. The bus came only once every half hour. It took him a few seconds to decide.

He decided to stay.

Within five minutes, the wheel was in place and the screws tightened. My father even helped the driver put the flat tire in the trunk. Then my father asked, "Are you by any chance heading towards Bnei Brak?"

"No," said the driver. "I'm going to Givat Shemuel. Why do you ask?"

"Because, as you saw, I missed my bus and I have an important class. I'll be late."

The driver shrugged his shoulders. "What can you do? So you'll be a little late."

"Maybe you'd be willing to pass Bnei Brak on your way to Givat Shemuel?" suggested my father. "It's on the way. From there you can cross the bridge and be there in a minute."

"But there's a traffic light on Rechov HaShomer," said the driver," and I'm in a big rush. I have to take the Geha highway. So, be well, and see you."

With that, he drove off.

We stood there at the bus stop. I looked at my father and his blackened hands from fixing the flat tire. I think I never saw him as shocked and puzzled as he was just then. He looked at me, and I think he saw the exact same thing in me (except for the dirty hands).

"What ingratitude," I said to him. My father didn't answer. "What an evil, ungrateful person. I hate him." My father didn't say anything.

"I never saw such an ungrateful person in my life. Why did he do that to you? What for?"

"You're shouting," said my father. "Talk quietly. Don't shout."

Suddenly I burst out crying. "Why did you help that evil man? Why did he treat you that way? How can anyone stand the way he acts? I never saw such ingratitude in my life."

I sat down on the bus stop bench crying bitterly. My father sat down next to me, looking sad and hurt. Yet what had happened seemed to affect me much more than it did him. My sense of justice was outraged at what I had seen, at that evil man and his evil deeds.

My father was sunk deep in thought. His eyes had a dreamy, far-away look to them.

Suddenly he smiled.

"Why are you smiling, Tatte?" I asked.

"It's not important. I just remembered that I once did see someone act with such a lack of gratitude."

"Who?"

"It would be *lashon hara*."

I knew I wouldn't be able to get the name out

of my father if it was a question of *lashon hara*. My father never said anything that you aren't allowed to say.

"Then at least tell me what happened," I said.

"It wasn't just one thing, it was dozens and maybe even hundreds of things," said my father. "And it wasn't just to one person, but to quite a few."

I found it hard to believe. "Are you telling me that you once saw a worse case of ingratitude than the one I just saw?"

"Absolutely," he said.

"Tell me at least one incident," I said. "Without names."

"Okay, I'll tell you," said my father. "But before I do, let me wash my hands in that store over there. I can't arrive at the *shiur* this way. On the other hand, maybe if they saw my hands, they'd forgive me for being late."

He crossed the road to the store and I was left at the bus stop waiting to hear his story about a worse case of ingratitude than what I had just seen. I didn't think such a thing was possible.

He returned and sat down next to me.

"I know someone who sat next to the sickbed of an ill person for weeks on end. He didn't even go to work. Instead, he took care of the sick person, fed him, changed his clothes, stayed up with him all night, studied with him and treated him with understanding even when the sick person lashed out angrily at him. Then, when the sick person got better, he didn't even say thank you or feel any appreciation for what the person had done for him.

"And not only that. After life returned to normal, the man asked the person who had been sick to do a small favor, to carry a small bag down a few flights of stairs. But the person didn't want to. When the man asked him again, the person who had been sick talked to him with such great chutzpah that it broke the man's heart."

"Who was it?" I asked before remembering that there was no chance my father would tell me.

"Which case of ingratitude is worse?" asked my father.

I thought about it. True, the story was only a story, while the incident with the driver was something I had seen with my own two eyes. But after giving it some thought, I had to admit that the ingratitude of the person who had been sick for several weeks was a worse case than the driver who was helped for ten minutes.

"There's another story I know firsthand," my father continued. "There was one boy who transferred to a new school and had a hard time adjusting to both the school work and his new classmates. The children teased him and he couldn't understand the subject matter. The boy was sad and depressed. His teacher decided to put a lot of time and effort into him. He studied with him, encouraged him, forgave him for a lot of foolish things he did, and succeeded in helping him improve in school work and socially as well. In fact, the boy turned into a class leader. Now how do you think he repaid his benefactor?"

"How?"

"Towards the end of the year he started getting the class to rebel against the teacher and call him names. What was lucky was that his classmates weren't as ungrateful as he was, so they didn't go along with it. The boy stopped his bad behavior but only after the principal sent him home for a couple of days to 'calm down.'

"The boy sat there for two days in the very same room where he had been sick for so many weeks with hepatitis. Over the two days he spent at home 'calming down,' he took out all his anger on his father and mother, the very people who raised him and educated him, who gave him everything, who barely slept a wink the whole time he was sick.

"But they weren't surprised by his in-gratitude. They were used to it, because he had always been that way. That same boy wasn't even willing to take down a bag of garbage when they asked him... Should I give you some more examples?"

"Enough, Tatte. I recognize the boy," I said.

Yup, it was me. I was the boy who was more ungrateful than that driver. I can't tell you how ashamed I felt there at the bus stop.

I remembered the long weeks I spent lying in bed sick with hepatitis. I remembered the devoted way my parents cared for me, the royal treatment they gave me, like at a 5-star hotel, and I felt ashamed, because till that very day they hadn't gotten a single word of thanks from me. As for my behavior, well, it's better not to talk about it.

The bus came. On the way to Bnei Brak, my father told me that if it would make me feel any better, a lot of kids are ungrateful without even realizing it.

"I don't have to tell you how much parents give their children from the minute they're born until they're married, and afterwards, too. Yet do they get anything for it?"

I didn't answer.

"The best children repay their parents by honoring them. They obey them, respect them, don't talk fresh to them, and try to bring them real *Yiddishe nachas*, by studying and praying the way they should and bringing home good grades and praise from the teacher. Average children don't always manage to bring their parents *nachas*, but at least they try to listen to them and not bring them anguish. But, there are a few children who — I don't know what to call them — but their actions are just like..."

He looked at me.

"That ungrateful driver," I said.

"I can't say that I blame you," he said. "Children think that the concept of 'gratitude' is only when it comes to strangers who do them a favor. They forget to look at the people closest to them, the people who do them endless favors from morning till night.

"Actually," added my father, "even if the parents didn't do the children any favors they would have to honor them. This is one of the Ten Commandments: 'Honor your father and your mother.' But when parents sacrifice so much for their children — and every parent does — then it's also a matter of ingratitude and lack of appreciation."

We got to where my father's *shiur* was held. It was a *Daf Yomi shiur*. My father apologized for coming late and briefly told everyone the reason. They grumbled out loud about the ungrateful driver and then my father decided to devote a few words to the subject of gratitude, which is the opposite of ingratitude. He told them this story:

Until ten years ago, there lived in Jerusalem a *tzaddik* named Rabbi Gustman, may his memory be a blessing, who was a *Rosh Yeshiva*. Once some of his students arrived at Rabbi Gustman's house and saw him watering the trees in the yard. Naturally, they felt uncomfortable at seeing the *Rosh Yeshiva* doing such work, and one of them suggested that the students do it. But Rabbi Gustman firmly told them that he would not allow anyone to steal the mitzvah of gratitude from him.

They were all astonished. What did gratitude have to do with watering the trees?

Rabbi Gustman told them, "As you all know, I was a very close student of the Torah giant and leader of the generation before the Holocaust, Rabbi Chaim Ozer Grodzinsky *ztz"l*. We used to talk in learning, arguing various points and lines of reasoning in the Gemara for hours.

"One day, as we talked, we walked through a forest. Suddenly Reb Chaim Ozer pointed to a certain plant and said to me, 'Do you see that? That plant must be avoided. Don't ever eat the leaves of that plant because they're poisonous.'

"I looked at him in astonishment. I was not known as someone given to eating plants for breakfast or any other meal. I didn't understand what he wanted from me.

"But Reb Chaim ignored my amazement and

went on to another plant. 'You can eat this plant without any qualms. The difference is in the stem. The poisonous one is green and this one is brown. Remember that.'

"I realized that Reb Chaim was not talking just to make conversation so I decided to participate. 'How do you eat a plant?' I asked. He explained to me what to do with the leaves, how to tear them into tiny pieces and mix them with water. He explained to me how to heat the leaves with fire or the sun, and gave details about what nutrients were contained in them. I couldn't get over the extent of his knowledge.

"The next day we again walked through the forest and he showed me dozens of plants, bushes, mushrooms, bark, and trees, of which some were not to be eaten and some were. He taught me signs to distinguish the poisonous plants from those good to eat. You might say I passed a short 'course' in plant identification, without having any idea why it was necessary.

"Three months later, the Germans overran the city and through Hashem's mercy I managed to escape to the forest along with several other students. After one day there, we were all starving. It was then that I first understood why the lessons had been so important.

"I started to examine the trees. I told my friends, 'Pick this one, but this one, don't even touch.' They looked at me as if I were crazy, but finally I concocted something and gave it to them to eat. They ate, felt satisfied, and even felt infused with new strength. Only then did I tell them how I became such an expert on plants.

"It was thanks to those plants that we survived, and *baruch Hashem* I made aliyah to *Eretz Yisroel* and have such wonderful *talmidim* — so wonderful that they will certainly not steal from me the mitzvah of gratitude to the Creator of the world and the plants He created that saved my life. Don't you think that watering the plants is a proper way to express my gratitude?"

My father's story made a deep impression on everyone. Then he asked their permission to tell another short story about Rabbi Gustman. Everyone agreed.

"When they put up a solar water heater on Rabbi Gustman's house, he noticed that his electricity bill went way down because he no longer had to turn on the electric hot water heater. Rabbi Gustman told an acquaintance that he owed thanks to the Creator, because it was thanks to the sun He created that he got this saving. In appreciation, Rabbi Gustman decided to add another half hour to his learning schedule, even though he was already busy learning most of the hours of the day."

Then my father told the people at the class, "I too owe thanks to Hashem for sending me the ungrateful driver who made such a strong impression on my beloved son, showing him how lowly such a character trait is and allowing him to realize the importance of gratitude. I hereby announce my vow to study an extra hour a day with my son, if he will only agree."

Everyone looked at me. Of course I agreed. The only question is, how can I ever repay my father for that wonderful surprise?

The Life Jacket

Meir's Story

The Life Jacket

About half a year ago my mother became very ill. She was in the hospital for a long time, and my father and older brothers looked very worried.

No one talked to me about my mother's illness. They must've thought I was too little. If you ask me, that was exactly why they should have talked to me, because I was very scared and worried. But they thought differently and just tried to hide whatever they could from me.

Like a lot of kids, though, I discovered ways of finding out what was going on — and what I heard was very bad. It was such a serious illness that my brothers didn't even want to say its name. One time I heard my big sister crying hard and saying into the telephone, "The doctors says it's hopeless." When I heard that, I got really scared. I knew that without a miracle, my mother would die in a few days and I would be left an orphan without any mother. I cried a long time and didn't have anyone to talk to or share my fears with.

This happened in Elul. In my *cheder* the teacher spoke of how "*teshuvah* and *tefillah* and *tzedakah* remove the evil of the decree." I listened carefully. He quoted: "Charity saves from death." Those words made a deep impression on me. I wanted to save my mother from death.

I went home and decided to give something of mine to charity. I didn't know what, though, because there were only a couple of dollars left in my piggy bank (that's because I'm no small spender). Suddenly, I remembered the clothing collection going on in our neighborhood in Jerusalem, where I live. It was run by none other than the wife of my principal, Rabbi Reichman. I opened my closet and, after a lot of indecision, finally decided to donate my winter jacket from the year before.

I went to my father with the jacket and told him that I wanted to donate it to charity. I told him that it was too small for me and that this year I could use my brother's old one.

My father asked me to try the jacket on again. I did. He said he thought I could wear it this year too, but I pleaded with him. "I want to give *tzedakah* so Mommy will get better. What difference does it make? I won't ask you to buy me a new jacket. I can get along fine with the old one. And besides, I'm the youngest in the family so there's no one after me to get the jacket."

My father agreed right away. "No problem," he said. "I hope this will help Mommy have a speedy recovery." I saw tears in his eyes when he said that.

I ran to the principal's house. His wife wasn't home, so he was the one who opened the door for me. I handed him the jacket and said that I wanted to donate it to *tzedakah*. He took one look at the coat and said, "It looks brand new. Are you sure your parents agreed to donate this?"

I explained to him that my mother couldn't agree because she was very sick and in the hospital. I told him that at first my father hadn't agreed, but that I convinced him to give the jacket to *tzedakah* to keep my mother from dying. My voice shook a little when I said that, and I saw that the principal was very moved.

"Rabbi Reichman, my mother will get better now, won't she?" I dared ask.

"We hope and pray," he said.

"I want you to promise me that my mother will get better," I said all of a sudden. I was shocked at my own courage. "Charity saves from death, doesn't it?"

The principal didn't know what to answer me. "Meir, you made a tremendous *hishtadlus* now. No one can promise things like that but I am certain that you contributed a great *z'chus* for your mother's recovery."

It sounded to me like the principal was trying to get out of it. I walked home disappointed and hurt. I wasn't sorry I gave the coat, but what I really wanted was for someone to tell me that my mother would definitely get better and not die.

The month of Elul passed. On Rosh Hashanah and Yom Kippur I prayed hard for my mother's recovery. She was still in the hospital and her condition kept getting worse. Sukkos was sad and boring. Most of the time neighbors watched us because the big kids were at the hospital with our mother.

It started raining right after Sukkos. My big sister took down the winter clothes. I wore a long-sleeved undershirt and sweater. When I left for school, I put on an old coat of my brother's. It looked big on me, but I didn't care.

A few days passed. It was freezing cold and pouring in Jerusalem. Those were difficult days because my mother's condition got a lot worse and the house was a total wreck. There was no one to wash our clothes. I wore the same things a few days in a row, so you can imagine how I looked.

It happened on a Tuesday, a day I'll never forget. School ended and I walked home, thinking hard about a lot of things. There was no reason for me to rush. No one was waiting for me anyway in the cold, sad house. I knew they were whispering very sad things in the house, things I didn't even want to hear. I refused to visit my mother because the last time I visited her made me really scared. I had bad dreams and cried all the time afterwards. I walked and felt my throat choke up and tears fill my eyes.

Suddenly I saw a group of boys standing in the middle of the sidewalk, next to a traffic sign. They were laughing and fooling around. It looked like they had decided to have some fun. They called out whatever they felt like at everyone who passed by. The one making the comments was Elazar, known for his great sense of humor.

The truth is that if I hadn't been so sad, I would have joined them. But I'm sure you can understand why I really didn't feel like it right then.

I stopped crying and tried to wipe the sad look off my face so I could pass by the group in peace. Just then I saw Elazar look at me gleefully, and I knew I had turned into a target.

"Look who's here — the beggar!" he said, and everyone burst out laughing. "Tell us, since when is a tent used for a coat?"

"What's your problem?" I said.

"You're the one who has a problem, not me," said Elazar. "Take a look at yourself and you'll see."

Without meaning to, I glanced down and saw he had a point. My shirt and pants were wrinkled and had mud stains on them. All that, plus the coat hanging on me as if I was a coat rack, really did make me look like a beggar.

I was deeply hurt.

"Believe me, if you'd hold out a hat, everyone would put money in it," said Elazar and everyone burst out laughing again. I just stared at him. I didn't have anything to answer back. He shot me a look and I lowered my gaze. Then, suddenly, I saw something that gave me a shock.

The lapels of his jacket looked very familiar. The fur trim belonged to the jacket...

Elazar was wearing my jacket!

My eyes went straight to the pocket. Yes, there was the small tear I recognized. It was my jacket, no doubt about it.

The discovery gave me back all my self-confidence. I knew that now I had it in my power to restore my self-respect and at the same time, put down Elazar. For a few seconds I pictured how I'd say to him, "Don't talk about beggars when you're wearing the jacket I donated to the clothing collection!" I knew that would shut him up. He wouldn't dare tease me after that.

But the words stuck in my throat. I felt it was too big a secret to reveal, that it was too much of a put-down. I knew that whatever I'd say would spread through the whole school, and that Elazar wouldn't be able to show his face in public.

I felt that Elazar's fate hung in the balance, that it depended on what I said — and I was afraid to condemn him.

I looked at Elazar. My lips trembled. Should I say it? Or keep quiet? Elazar was still smiling. He said, "Just give me a percentage of the money you collect, okay?"

I kept on looking at him and he started to feel uncomfortable. "What are you looking at me like that for? I don't have a penny to give you — beggar."

Someone else heard that last word. It was Rabbi Reichman, who just then passed by on his way home.

"What did you say?" We heard his voice and spun around. "Repeat what you just said!"

Elazar didn't say a word.

"I want you to repeat immediately what you just said!" the principal commanded sharply.

"I said...beggar," Elazar blurted out.

The principal looked at me. I saw him look at the shabby coat, and then I saw a flash of recognition before he quickly turned back to

Elazar. I saw his gaze focus on Elazar's coat.

He recognized it. He couldn't have not recognized it because he had talked to me about how the coat looked so new.

He looked at me, then at Elazar, then back again at me. Lots of thoughts passed through his mind. I could hear what he was thinking.

"And what did you answer him?" he finally asked me.

"I didn't answer him anything," I said looking directly into the principal's eyes as hard as I could.

I saw his face light up. I saw great admiration on his face, and at the same time, an expression of relief.

"Go home, Elazar," the principal said sternly. "You may not know this, but Meir's mother is very ill. I hope that you and your friends will never, ever be in his situation. Come see me tomorrow in my office and tell me what punishment you deserve — even though what I just told you should be punishment enough."

I looked at Elazar's face. He looked miserable. He hadn't known my mother was sick and now he was embarrassed in front of his friends. He hung his head and mumbled, "I'm sorry. I didn't know."

"As for you, Meir," said Rabbi Reichman, "please come with me to the office right now. I want to have a few words with you."

I went with him, the coat dragging on me. I

thought I knew what he was going to say to me. But I was wrong.

I went into his office. He sat down in his chair looking thunderstruck. He started talking and the words came tumbling out fast. "I'm shocked. It's hard for me to believe I have a boy like this in our school. Tell me something, how did you hold yourself back from answering? Even grownups wouldn't have been able to stand up to the pressure," he said.

I answered.

"Did you recognize the coat?" he asked, just to be sure.

I nodded my head yes.

"What made you keep quiet and not say a thing?"

I shrugged my shoulders. "I don't know. I thought it would be...too much. I thought..."

"I can't imagine even an adult passing that test," said the principal. He paused for a minute, thinking. "Actually, though, there is someone who did. It happened a long time ago. Take a look at him."

The principal pointed to a picture on the wall. It was the portrait of a man.

"Who's that?" I asked.

"His name is Rabbi Avraham Bardaki. He was the principal of the famous Jerusalem Talmud Torah HaMesorah for many years. He was the only one...and now you."

Suddenly, he remembered something. "Listen, Meir, do you remember when you asked me to promise you that your mother would get better and I didn't agree?"

"Sure I remember," I said, but I didn't quite get the connection.

"Now I'm almost positive she will get better. Don't look at me like that. I'm not a prophet. It's all because of him," he said, pointing to the portrait of Rabbi Avraham Bardaki.

Now I was really confused.

"Sit down and I'll tell you," said Rabbi Reichman. I sat down across from him and he began.

"Rabbi Avraham Bardaki was not only a school principal, he was an outstanding educator as well. He was truly great, great in Torah. When he was 75, a problem developed in one of his feet, and after a series of tests, the doctors told him there was no choice but to amputate the foot.

"He went home downcast, thinking about no longer being able to walk through the school and visit all the classes. He turned sad at the thought of all the people he would have to put to the trouble of pushing him in a wheelchair. He walked home with aching feet and an aching heart.

"As he approached the building he lived in, he encountered a very arrogant man who lived on the block. The man began by saying to him, 'You're someone who is negligent about cleanliness. Because of your building, the whole street is filthy. How can you be like that? Why are you dirtying the whole street?'

"Rabbi Avraham could have answered that he and his wife were elderly, and that they were meticulous about cleanliness. But he chose to remain silent while the arrogant man continued to blame him and humiliate him.

"When the man saw that his words weren't getting any reaction, he ended his tirade with one particularly sharp insult and left.

"Then Rabbi Avraham said to one of his students who met him there, 'That must have been instead of the foot.'

"The student didn't understand what he meant until a few days later when the doctors notified Rabbi Avraham that the infection had healed and there was no longer any need to amputate his foot.

"To his friends, Rabbi Avraham explained that there was no estimating the size of the reward for those who 'are humiliated yet do not humiliate in return, who hear themselves shamed, yet do not reply. About them it is written: "Hashem loves them with the strength of a strong sun." ' Such people are especially beloved by Hashem and He doesn't want anything bad to happen to those He loves.

"My dear Meir," said the principal, "you too are one of Hashem's beloved. You were shamed and you could have answered back yet you chose to remain silent. The humiliation you suffered must have come in place of a greater suffering. Now I am almost certain that Hashem will heal your mother."

"I hope so," I said, bursting into tears. The principal comforted me, repeating over and over again, "It'll be all right, Meir, it'll be all right." He emphasized that he wasn't promising me that my mother would get better but only that it seemed very, very much that way to him.

Two months have passed since then and you're probably anxious to know what happened.

I'll tell you. The doctors held out no hope at all for my mother. On the recommendation of one of the *gedolei hador*, she was flown to America, where she underwent very difficult treatments. There were times of despair and times of hope, and in the end...

This week my mother came home. She's thin and very weak, but she's recovered from her serious illness. Now I'm sitting here in my room quietly, so that I won't bother her while she's resting, and I'm writing this story. I think there's a lot to learn from it.

I made up with Elazar. He apologized with his

whole heart and we worked it out. Every time we pass the street sign I think, "Thank You for the miracle You made for me here," and imagine to myself what would have been if I had answered him back. I would never have known what I lost out on.

And when I sit next to my mother, I'm so happy to be with her. I know for sure that I'll always belong to those who "are humiliated yet do not humiliate in return, who hear themselves shamed, yet do not reply."

Be My Friend

Yossi's Story

Be My Friend

I was born in Bnei Brak. I lived there my whole life, eleven years, until I started school this year.

During summer vacation we moved to Jerusalem.

To tell you the truth, the move to Jerusalem came as no surprise to me. My father was born in Jerusalem. Ever since I can remember, my father used to tell us that the day would come when we'd move to Jerusalem. Every vacation, the whole family would take a trip to Jerusalem to visit the *Kosel* and the narrow streets of Me'ah She'arim. I've always loved Jerusalem and couldn't wait for the day when we'd live there.

A month before the move, I read a book about a boy whose family went to America and who couldn't take the pain of saying goodbye. The book left me feeling worried. I was afraid it would be hard for me to adjust, too. I knew that when we moved I would have to say goodbye to my friends, and I'm a pretty sociable kid. But when the day of the move arrived, I discovered that I was different than the boy described in the book. I guess I'm not that sensitive, because even though I felt sad about leaving my friends, I also felt happy that the day I had dreamed about for so long had finally arrived.

I pictured myself as a "Yerushalmi." I was happy that I'd be able to visit the Kosel whenever I wanted and that we'd be living right next to Me'ah She'arim, the neighborhood I like to visit best. For me, the move was as easy as pie.

But with all the thinking and dreaming I forgot one thing. I forgot that in Jerusalem, besides the Kosel and the nice neighborhoods, there are also kids I'd have to make friends with.

At the beginning of the school year, I entered a large, famous *cheder*. The night before the first day of school, I felt slightly tense. For the first time, I thought about all the kids I didn't even know, and suddenly I realized that I'd have to start all over again from the beginning. This time, it wasn't just the regular beginning of a new school year, where I'd go back and meet my friends; it was joining a class where not a single one of the kids knew me.

I started worrying, but calmed myself down with the thought that there was no reason for it to be any different from last year. After all, I hadn't changed — and I had never had any problems making friends.

It only took me a few days to realize how wrong I was.

It wasn't that anyone fought with me or anything like that. It was just that the kids ignored me, as if I was one of the desks in the classroom.

The first day, I found a place at the back of the room. I sat there alone. During recess, I looked at the boys huddled in the center of the classroom talking about what had happened to them over summer vacation. Except for two boys who said hello to me and another two who asked me where I was from, not a single boy came over to me, and no one asked my name or paid any attention to me.

At first I thought they were just shy. But it didn't take me long to see that they were far from being anything like that. On the other hand, I didn't think they were bad kids, either. They didn't bother me or fight with me. They just ignored me, as if I was invisible — as if I didn't even exist.

One week passed, and then another. There I was, sitting surrounded by a whole classroom of kids, yet it was as if four invisible walls separated me from them. It was unbelievable. I had never felt so alone. In fact, I had never, ever felt lonely before in my life.

Sometimes I'd wander around during recess, trying to get their attention. It didn't work. Once I tried to join in a conversation. They looked at me and suddenly stopped talking. They didn't laugh at me or tease me, they just looked at me with polite surprise. They felt uncomfortable having me listen to their conversation — as if I was their teacher, or as if I was some strange kid sticking his nose into other people's business.

That day on the way home, I saw my classmates walking in groups, talking excitedly about whatever, while I walked by myself, totally alone. Something like this had never happened to me before. Tears started to spill down my cheeks, tears that turned into real crying that wouldn't stop. I turned my head to the side so that they wouldn't see I was crying, and ran home.

Sitting in my room, I realized that my mad dash home had been totally unnecessary. There was no way they would have noticed I was crying. They just weren't interested in me.

The days went by fast. Every so often I'd talk with a kid in class. The conversations were short and casual — with me usually being the one to start them. If a boy happened to ask me for a pencil or pen, I'd jump for joy, thinking he wanted to be my friend. But it wasn't long before I found out that all he wanted was something to write with, not my friendship.

It was a tough time for me. For some reason, I didn't say anything to my parents, maybe because I didn't want to spoil their happiness. I guess, if you want to know the truth, I was ashamed. I saw my brothers and sisters getting along fine, while here I was, me the *chevra'man* of the family, without any friends. I asked myself whether I had just happened to end up in a class like that, or whether I was the one to blame.

Two months passed. Two full months during which I stopped even trying to talk to any of the kids in my class. Sure I talked — but not to make friends. Not even a little.

One day our teacher didn't come to school and a substitute came instead.

I noticed how happy the boys in my class were. Of course, that didn't necessarily mean anything, because kids are always happy when a substitute comes. It's a nice change from the routine. As for me, I couldn't have cared less one way or the other. What difference did it make who taught me if I didn't even feel like being in the class?

The substitute, whose name was Reb Yosef, looked at us. You could see he knew each and every boy in the class quite well. We waited to see what he would say.

He started talking about things that had happened the last time he was in the class, the year before. From what I could understand, he had been in the middle of a story last year. Now the kids asked him to finish it. He looked around the classroom, his eyes moving from boy to boy. He had something to say to practically each one.

Then he looked at me.

"I see we have a new student in class," Reb Yosef declared.

He kept looking at me. I felt that he was concentrating on my expression, not just staring for no good reason.

I lowered my eyes. He came over to me and asked me straight out, "Tell me something — did they give you a nice welcome here?"

I was shocked by the directness of the question. A teacher I didn't even know, in the classroom for only five minutes, suddenly hits me with a question like that — one that's been bothering me ever since I came into the class. His simple question touched all the pain I was keeping inside.

I burst out crying. All the boys turned around to look at me in surprise. From their expressions I realized that they had absolutely no idea of the reason for my tears. I kept on crying. The teacher bent down next to me and asked me a few questions. I didn't answer. I couldn't. Besides, what was the point in saying anything when my sobs said it all?

I put my head down on the desk and covered it with my arm. In the meantime, I listened to the discussion that took place in the classroom.

Reb Yosef asked some plain and simple questions. He asked the boys who I was and where I came from. Only a few boys knew. He started to ask if they included me in their games. His voice became more and more stern. I felt relieved that someone finally noticed my suffering, that someone was reminding my classmates that a new boy had joined them.

At the end of his brief investigation, Reb Yosef began rebuking my classmates. He described to them exactly how a boy feels when he comes into a new class — about his fears and worries, and how he feels when no one pays any attention to him. He described perfectly what I had been feeling since the beginning of the year. It was as if he had gotten inside my heart and read what was written there.

"Because of what I've seen here today," said Reb Yosef, "I will not continue the story I began last time."

The whole class groaned in disappointment but then Reb Yosef added, "Instead, I will tell you about Hagaon Harav Moshe Feinstein *ztz"l*."

A sigh of satisfaction was heard. It didn't matter what story it was, as long as there'd be a story.

Once, Rabbi Moshe Feinstein, who was the leader of Torah-true Jewry in America, went to a wedding. He was the *mesader kiddushin*. When the ceremony was over, people came over to shake his hand and ask for a blessing.

Reb Moshe, as he was affectionately called, was in a very big rush because he had to get to another wedding, yet he took the time to shake everyone's hand, all the while smiling his famous smile.

His driver gently urged the crowd to let him leave. "The Rav needs to get to another wedding," the driver called out in a gravelly voice, but the people there kept crowding around the sage to ask for a blessing.

It took a while until the driver was finally able to escort Reb Moshe to the exit. The whole way, people at the wedding followed him, asking for blessings and advice. Finally, Reb Moshe entered the car. The driver, who kept glancing at his watch, rushed to start the engine. He had just pulled away from the parking lot when suddenly he heard a cry.

"Stop!"

He stopped with a screech. "What happened?"

"I must go back to the hall," said Reb Moshe.

"If something has been left behind, I can go up and get it," said the driver.

"No," insisted Reb Moshe. "I must go back myself."

The driver, seeing how adamant Reb Moshe was, parked the car and accompanied him back to the hall.

When they went in, the driver saw that Reb Moshe began to scan the hall for someone.

"Who are you looking for?" he asked.

"I don't know," answered Reb Moshe.

The driver wondered a little about that answer but didn't say anything. He knew there must be something to it.

After several minutes of looking, Reb Moshe suddenly spotted the person he was looking for. He crossed the hall quickly, never taking his eyes off the person for fear of losing him. When he reached him he said, "*Shalom aleichem*, Reb Yid. How are you? How do you feel?" The man was startled. He couldn't understand the meaning of this special attention, yet it was easy to see how pleased he was by it.

Finally Reb Moshe asked, "What is your name?" The stranger answered. Reb Moshe then parted from him with a great display of affection.

When they were once again seated in the car,

the driver respectfully asked Reb Moshe the meaning of what had happened and who the man was. The driver was certain he must be a hidden *tzaddik*.

Reb Moshe told him that he had never seen the man before in his life. "Quite simply," answered Reb Moshe, "this man was one of the guests who asked for my blessing just as I was concentrating on the door of the elevator not closing on me. I nodded goodbye to him. I didn't look at him, nor did I smile at him. I was preoccupied with something else. When we started driving away, I remembered his look of disappointment at not receiving a radiant countenance from me. That's why I went back and looked for his face, which I remembered, and gave him the attention he deserved. As our Sages say: 'Greet every person with a radiant countenance.' "

The teacher ended his story. The kids in the class got the message, but the teacher wasn't finished yet.

"You have no idea how important it is for a person to be treated decently, to be paid attention to. Hagaon Harav Shlomo Wolbe *shlita* told his students that sometimes boys meet their friends on the way to shul. There are some who say "good morning" in a warm way, with feeling. But there are others who say the same words indifferently.

The first restore life to the one who hears them and probably make him learn that day with enthusiasm and joy, while the latter put the one who hears them in a bad mood — all because one boy didn't greet his friend with a radiant countenance.

"There is a boy sitting here in this class for close to two months and not a single person has shown him a radiant countenance. No one has paid any attention to him. Do any of you know what that can do to a boy? I am sure that some of you, and perhaps all of you, have exchanged a few words with him. But has anyone ever shown him a radiant countenance? Has anyone ever greeted him with a friendly smile, as each person should be greeted?"

All the kids in class were silent. You could see they were sorry.

"I am sure you did not act this way on purpose," said the teacher. Then he turned to me. "I know this class. Believe me, these boys have good hearts. The problem is that they're still children and don't always think. Forgive them, and I promise you they won't treat you that way again."

I nodded my head to indicate that I forgave them.

Reb Yosef continued to tell us stories about showing other people a radiant countenance.

Some of the stories were really amazing. He also gave us some ideas of how to show a radiant countenance to our friends, our brothers and sisters, and even our parents. He vividly portrayed for us the feelings of a person when he is greeted with a radiant countenance.

"It is written: 'White teeth are better than giving milk to drink,'" said the teacher. "A person who smiles at his friend and shows him 'white teeth' (here the teacher smiled to reveal two rows of white teeth; we laughed) is better than someone who gives him milk to drink."

He told about the great *mashgiach* Rabbi Chaim Friedlander *ztz"l* who used to talk to every person with a big smile on his face. What was really interesting was that he used to smile even when he talked on the telephone. When asked why he did it, he explained that even on the telephone you can feel if a person is speaking to you with a smile.

To give us a sense of how it feels, the teacher turned around so we couldn't see his face. Then he talked. To our surprise, we could tell when he was smiling and when he wasn't.

The more stories he told, the more the atmosphere in the class improved. The teacher spoke his words of rebuke with a radiant countenance and sugar-coated them in a pleasant atmosphere, so everyone accepted what he said.

I won't make my story too long. From that day on, my problem was solved. It disappeared as if it had never existed. Everyone made friends with me without any problem. A lot of the kids apologized and explained to me that they just weren't thinking. They assured me that they hadn't meant anything bad. It just came from not paying attention.

There's an end to this story, just like there was a beginning.

This week a new boy came into our class. He transferred from a different school in Jerusalem. What do you think I did the minute he walked into our class?

Restored to Life

Aryeh's Story

Restored to Life

This week there was a terrible accident here in Tiberius where I live. Avi, one of my best friends, was crossing the street in the pedestrian crosswalk when suddenly a car came and hit him. He was killed on the spot. The car drove off.

Everyone was very sad — all the boys in the *cheder*, who knew him well, and all our neighbors. It was very hard for me to sleep at night. I dreamed about him and even imagined that it was happening to me. I woke up with my face covered with sweat. I'm also a little scared when I picture what's happening to Avi right now. I also miss him a lot, even though I wasn't his best friend.

Yesterday I sat on the front porch of my house. With me were my friend from school, David (we're in the fourth grade), and my brother

Yossi. We talked about the terrible accident that happened to Avi.

"I wonder where he is now," said David.

"He's in heaven, in *Gan Eden*. It's good for him there."

"But we're sad here," said Yossi. "For Avi it's good, but he left us feeling sad."

I didn't have anything to answer so I kept quiet.

"But Avi isn't to blame," I said finally, wanting to defend his memory.

"So who is to blame?" I suddenly heard a voice say from behind us.

It was my grandfather, who had been sitting behind us the whole time in the lounge chair, quietly listening to our conversation.

None of us said a thing. I mean, you couldn't blame...

"No one is to blame," said my grandfather. "Hashem sends a soul down to this world and He decides when to take him back. Sometimes Hashem wants people to repent and so He takes the soul of someone beloved, and that makes everyone think about whether they can improve their behavior. But there are some people who, instead of that, look to see who is to blame."

We felt ashamed.

"Wait a minute," I said. "Then why do we pray for the sick person to get better? Why don't we just say, 'Hashem decided and that's it!' "

"Hashem decrees a decree and he can also cancel it, if people repent. You yourselves know that there are a lot of very sick people who get better. That happens when Hashem sees that people repent before the decree is enacted."

"But," said Yossi, "but...Avi didn't..." He stopped in the middle.

"Go ahead and ask. Don't be embarrassed," said my grandfather. Yossi didn't want to ask, but when I realized what he wanted to ask, I decided to do it myself.

"Grandpa," I said, "Avi didn't have a chance to be saved from the decree because he died the second he was hit, so there was no chance for his family or friends to repent. He wasn't sick or anything like that, he was just...killed" — I choked on the words — "and that's it. There's no way to bring him back."

"Are you sure there's no way?" my grandfather asked.

"Is it possible to bring back someone who died?" I asked.

"Didn't you ever hear about 'revival of the dead'?" my grandfather asked me back.

"That's only when *Mashiach* comes," I said.

"First of all, what do you mean by 'only'?" said my grandfather indignantly. "Isn't *Mashiach* coming today? If everyone repents, *Mashiach* will

come today. It all depends on us. That's one of
the fundamentals of belief. And if we don't
believe in it enough, then we have a big problem.

"Besides," my grandfather said suddenly,
"even before *Mashiach* comes there have been
incidents of revival of the dead."

"Why didn't we hear about them?" persisted
Yossi.

"We did hear about them," I said. "We learned
in *Navi* about Elisha who brought a boy back to
life."

"My grandson knows something," noted my
grandfather, who didn't usually give out
compliments. I blushed.

"And now, if I tell you that I, Yechiel ben
Gittel, saw with my own eyes an act of reviving
the dead, would you believe me?"

We didn't answer. I looked at David and
Yossi. What could I say? Their faces certainly
didn't look too believing. Yet I knew that my
grandfather wasn't the type of person who just
talks for nothing.

Then my elderly grandfather closed his eyes
and started to tell us one of the most amazing
stories I've ever heard in my whole life. I'm going
to tell it to you, but before I do, it's important to
me that you promise to believe me when I tell
you that this story is one hundred percent true!

"It happened on Lag b'Omer 75 years ago, in

5683 ('23)," my grandfather began. "I was then a boy of sixteen, and I lived here in Tiberias. That's how it is, once a Tiberian always a Tiberian.

"Every Lag b'Omer we used to travel with Foiglander to Meron. Foiglander was none other than an old donkey whose owner, one of the wagon drivers in Tiberias, decided to name him after a Count who once harmed his grandfather. It seems he felt that if it was decreed that he hit someone with a whip, better it should be 'Foiglander'."

We burst out in such peals of rolling laughter that Grandpa had to threaten to stop telling his story unless we stopped laughing.

"That year, Lag b'Omer came out on Saturday night so we set out for Meron on Friday, hoping to arrive by noon so that we'd have time to get ready for Shabbos. That same skinny animal barely managed to pull the wagon that my brother, the wagon driver, and I sat on. By a miracle we somehow managed to get to Meron, even arriving there before noon, as we had planned.

"We weren't the only ones who got there. Hundreds and thousands of people congregated in Meron each year to go up to the burial site of Rabbi Shimon bar Yochai on his *yahrzeit*. The roads then weren't paved; still, thousands came.

"Shabbos began. Each person found himself a

place to stay and, believe me, in those days there weren't hotels or guest houses. Anyone who had a roof over his head and even a thin blanket was happy with his lot. Actually, so was someone who didn't have all that.

"The amazing incident I'm about to tell you happened on Shabbos morning, after *Musaf*, in the study hall next to the *kever* of the Rashbi, in the last minyan closest to noon. Suddenly we heard loud sounds of shouting and crying. We ran to where the noise was coming from and saw a huge crowd surrounding a boy who lay on the ground without a breath of life in him.

"At that time, there was an epidemic raging that cut down quite a few people. The disease was so contagious that the government would take anyone who came into contact with a dead person and put him into quarantine for several days, so that he wouldn't pass it on further.

"All of a sudden someone cried, 'Government officials are coming!' We all scattered, running away for fear that we would be locked up in a building in quarantine for several days.

"The panic was awful. People tried to escape every which way while the government officials used their combined efforts to close the gates. My ten-year-old brother managed to get outside.

"I was left inside.

"The boy's body was resting in one of the

small rooms built on top. You didn't need a doctor to see that the boy had died from the epidemic. He was completely green, and the doctors who came to check him decided to prevent all the people there from leaving.

"When the order was heard inside, an anguished cry arose. It seems that mothers were trapped inside, with their three-year-old sons left all alone outside, without any friends or relatives. I myself was worried that my little brother wouldn't know what to do. Next to me a man shouted that he had left his one-year-old son lying in a cradle in a tent far from the *kever* and that now the child would die because no one would know of his existence. Still, the non-Jewish government officials refused to budge. They stood guard on both sides of the gate to make sure no one left.

"The wailing increased. The policemen promised they would try to find the children outside and so managed to calm the worried crowd slightly. But then we heard the wails of the poor woman whose three-year-old son had died. 'This is my one and only son, my firstborn. I vowed to make him a *chalaka* on the *kever* of the *tzaddik* and now he is gone. Dead! Dead! Dead!' She cried and tore out her hair, and the crowd broke out weeping for her tragedy.

"We were too sad and anguished to make

Kiddush on the wine and eat our Shabbos meal.
The joy turned to mourning and sadness, and I,
only sixteen at the time, didn't know what to do.
I worried about what would happen to my
brother and what would happen to me. I worried
that maybe I would catch the disease and die too,
chas v'shalom."

My grandfather paused in his story and took a
deep breath. You could see he was deeply moved
even though so many years had passed since
then. We sat there holding our breaths, waiting
to hear the rest of the story.

"Suddenly," my grandfather continued, "the
boy's mother stood up and dramatically picked
the dead boy up in her arms and started to carry
him downstairs, to the shul. The policemen, and
even some of the other people there, began shouting at her to put him down, but no one dared get
too close to her for fear of contagion.

"We followed her quietly, careful to keep our
distance. She walked over to the *kever* until she
was right next to it, put the dead boy on the floor,
and in a bitter, sobbing voice cried out these
exact words:

'O *tzaddik, tzaddik* Rabbi Shimon! Here
stands your loyal daughter. I came here to you to
cut the hair of my only son, to bring him here on
Lag b'Omer. Yesterday I brought him here alive
and made his *chalaka* with songs and music,

with tambourine and violin, with feasting and joy. How can I leave here now without my only son? How will I return home alone?'

"The sound of her weeping was heard in every part of the room. There wasn't a single heart that didn't break upon hearing the cries of that heart-broken woman. I cried too, and took it upon myself then and there to be more dedicated to Torah and learning if only a miracle would occur.

"But the boy didn't move a muscle. Everyone pitied the woman, knowing that what was done could not be undone.

"After she finished crying and pleading, she stood up and said, '*Tzaddik, tzaddik*, I am placing him here before you as he is. Please do not shame me and leave me empty-handed. Pray that he be returned to me alive and well, as I brought him here yesterday. Sanctify the Name of Heaven in the world so all will know that there is a God Who rules the world.'

"After that she turned around. She went out of the shul and asked everyone to do the same. We went out and left the body of the boy inside.

"We waited expectantly. A tense silence pervaded. All was absolutely still.

"After a few minutes of quiet, a weak voice was heard coming from inside the shul. We put our ears to the door and heard clearly the voice of a child calling for his mother. We rushed to open the door and right before our eyes we saw the boy stand up on his own two feet and cry, 'Imma, give me a drink. I'm thirsty.'

"The mother fell upon him with hugs and kisses. In the excitement we forgot to bring him water, until he asked again and then everyone ran to bring him water.

"The boy's mother took him upstairs. It's hard to describe the excitement and happiness we all felt at the revival of the dead boy. The whole crowd gathered close to see the boy now alive and well. The doctors pushed their way through the crowd to check the boy. They admitted it was a miracle. They allowed the gates to be opened immediately, without further delay, for there was no longer any need for a quarantine.

"It was a great sanctification of God's Name, and all those present, myself included, who saw the miracle with our own eyes, made the blessing '*mechayei hameisim.*' "

My grandfather finished his thrilling story, looked at us and said, "I, who saw with my own two eyes an instance of revival of the dead, want my grandson and the whole world to know and believe that there is no decree that is impossible to rescind. Look — the mother's tears annulled the terrible decree and restored a dead boy to life. In the same way, every terrible decree can be cancelled. It all depends on us."

I decided to write you this great story that made me believe even more in the revival of the dead so that you would believe, too.

My grandfather promised to take me this Lag b'Omer to the *kever* of Rabbi Shimon bar Yochai in Meron to show me exactly where the boy died, where they carried him, and exactly where he came back to life. My grandfather said that even though they changed the building, he can still identify the exact spot where the great miracle of the revival of the dead happened.

So if you come to Meron this year and see a boy walking alongside a very old man, you'll know it's me and my grandfather. He'll be telling me again what happened 75 years ago, and you can come along with us. Everything will be just like then, except for one missing thing that will keep the picture from being complete.

The old donkey — Foiglander.

I wrote that so you'd finish the story with a smile on your face.

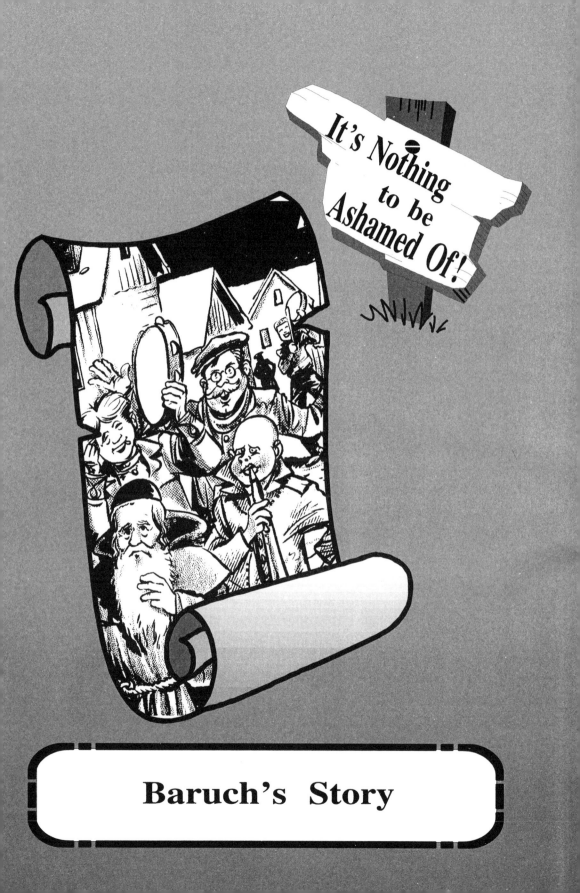

It's Nothing to be Ashamed Of!

Baruch's Story

It's Nothing to be Ashamed Of!

I'm in the fourth grade and live in Netanya. I wanted to tell you a little about my father.

My father works half a day in an office and the other half, he studies Torah.

Everyone knows my father and they all like him a lot because he has a good heart. He's smart, too, and he helps everyone.

Still, there were some kids who didn't know how to appreciate my father, and who even hurt my feelings about him. And that's what I want to tell you about.

When my father walks down the street, he always carries various shopping bags of all colors filled with food. Lots of times you can see my father loading stoves and refrigerators, tables

and chairs, washing machines and even bunk
beds onto a truck.

Besides that, he's the one who puts back all
the books everyone leaves lying around the study
hall. And if that's still not enough, there was the
time when a friend of mine and I were walking to
school and we saw my father trying to open a
clogged drain in the building my friend lives in.

My friends don't laugh at me, but they ask me
questions that embarrass me, like, "Is your
father the caretaker of the shul? Is he a moving
man? Is he a plumber? How much food do you
need?"

I tell them the truth, that my father works in
an office and learns in the afternoon — but they
don't believe me. After all, they see him putting
the books back all the time. And isn't the one who
does that the shul's caretaker? Who loads all
sorts of closets onto a truck if not a moving man?
Who cleans a drain if not a plumber?

One day I told my father what my friends
were saying and he laughed and said that he
really was a caretaker, plumber and all those
things. At the end he said, "And don't forget to
remind your friends that I'm also a cook." (My
father also knows how to cook.)

But the truth is that my father does
everything for free, for the mitzvah. He brings
the food he cooks to the homes of the old and

needy. (Sometimes he sends me to deliver it). If a young couple gets married and needs furniture, my father finds someone who wants to get rid of his old furniture and then he brings it to the people who need it. In the building my friend lives in, there's an old man my father helps. Once when he had a clogged drain, instead of calling a plumber, he called my father — because a plumber costs money and he (my father) does it for free.

Lots of times I've gone with my father on his visits to sick people and people who are all alone. He always leaves them a thermos and plastic containers filled with hot food, and after that he talks to them. Sometimes I listen in. It doesn't take me long to figure out why the person needs my father's help. Lots of times, though, my father talks in Yiddish, a language I don't understand at all, except for a word or two here and there.

What I do understand is that sometimes my father doesn't get any thank-you for his trouble. Worst of all is that there are some needy people who shout at him and say he doesn't know how to cook. That's not true. He does know how. And besides, my father is doing them a favor, so why are they shouting at him?

But that's besides the point. What really hurt me was what my friends thought. Their fathers wear suits and ties, and I always had the feeling that maybe my friends looked down a little on my father, who doesn't dress that way.

On the one hand, I was really proud of my father, that he's such a wonderful person and does such important mitzvos. But on the other hand, I felt uncomfortable.

One day this week after school my father asked me to help him take clothes from an old lady who wanted to give them to the poor.

I was glad to go with him. When we got to the apartment, we saw right away that the clothes were so torn and tattered that no one would wear them. Actually, they didn't even look like clothes. They looked more like rags, like the ones my mother uses to clean windows. I said that to my father and he agreed with me, but to my surprise he started to collect the clothes anyway and take them downstairs.

I also picked up a pile of "rags" and ran down the stairs after him.

"Abba," I asked, "why don't you tell her we don't need them?"

"*Chas v'chalila*," said my father. "She called specially, because she wanted to do a mitzvah. We mustn't disappoint her."

We put the clothes in the pickup truck my father rented (his driver gave us a strange look, as if he was wondering what we needed those rags for) and we went back upstairs. There was a whole roomful of clothes to empty out.

"It seems to me that she just wanted to get rid of all her junk for free and that's why she called you," I said. "Just like the old man and the plumber."

My father stopped dead in his tracks, looked at me in astonishment, and then asked, "Why do you sound so angry?"

I didn't know what to answer, so I kept quiet.

My father looked at me for another couple of seconds and then went back upstairs, with me following behind him.

We went up and down a few more times. We were sweating from the heavy loads. That was normal, but what made the work seem doubly hard to me was knowing that all those rags were going straight into the garbage.

The fourth or fifth time I went down, as I left the building and headed for the pickup truck, I saw a group of my classmates walking down the block. I didn't waste too much time thinking. I raced back inside the building, bumped right into the huge pile of clothes my father was carrying, and said, "Abba, wait a minute! Don't go out."

He looked at me. "What happened?"

I didn't know how to put it. "Look, Abba, my friends are passing by. I don't want them to see us carrying clothes."

My father looked at me and I looked at him. I

saw his face turn angry, and then I burst out crying.

I cried like I hadn't cried in years. All the pain inside me, that I didn't know how to express, poured out. My father looked at me in surprise, but I kept on sobbing.

He put the pile down on the side of the hall and put his hand on my shoulder. "Don't worry," he said gently. "If that's what you want, I won't go out. I'll wait until they pass. Don't worry."

He stepped outside (without the pile) a few times until he finally announced, "The coast is clear. They're gone. Do I have your permission to continue the mitzvah?"

The question made me feel ashamed. A father doesn't need to ask his son what to do. My father wanted to make sure I realized how strange my request was.

We did the rest of the work in silence, until we finished collecting every last article of clothing donated by the old lady. My father thanked her warmly for her great generosity (as he put it), and she said that although it was hard for her to part with the clothes, she gave them because she knew that my father needed them a lot, etc., etc.

We got in the truck. The driver asked, "To where?" When he heard my father's answer, he raised his eyebrows.

After we finished throwing everything into a

big garbage can several blocks away, the driver asked my father, "Why did you need to go so far? Couldn't you have thrown it all into the garbage cans near the building?"

My father explained to him that he didn't want to hurt the lady's feelings. I saw the driver's expression change. Unless I'm wrong, I think I saw something glisten in his eyes. He didn't say anything. He just drove us home in silence.

We got out of the pickup truck and my father asked, "What do I owe you?"

"Nothing," said the driver.

We looked at him. "What do you mean, nothing?" said my father. "What's the cost of the four hours?"

"Nothing," repeated the driver. "I'm not taking any money from you."

"This is a new one," said my father. "You worked, take what's coming to you."

The driver shut the engine. "Look," he said, "I don't wear a *kippa* and I've never gone to shul in my life except for Yom Kippur. I never liked the religious and sometimes I even hated them. But after what I saw today, I take off the hat I don't wear to you." He paused. "I envy you. I've driven plenty of folks in this truck but I'm real glad a wonderful person like you has sat in it. I should pay *you* money for traveling with me. Don't even dream of trying to pay me."

My father started to protest, but the driver started the engine and began to drive away. Suddenly he stopped and shouted, "When you need me again for something like this, give me a call. I'll drop everything and come for free." He tossed out his business card and drove off.

I stood there and looked at my father. I saw a broad smile on his face, a smile that turned into real laughter. He came closer to me, put his hand on my shoulder and said, "See? We may have lost the mitzvah of giving *tzedakah*, but we gained two other mitzvos: We brought pleasure to a lonely widow, and we also had the merit of sanctifying Hashem's Name."

I stood there feeling very uncomfortable. It was hard for me to remember that just half an hour ago I had been ashamed of such a wonderful father.

We went home. By now, it was nighttime and I went right to bed. I was thinking over everything that happened, especially what the driver said, when all of a sudden, my father came into the room and sat down on the edge of my bed.

"Baruch, your crying today taught me that you've been carrying a heavy burden in your heart for quite some time. I understand your feelings. You might want your father to be special and distinguished and not run around with shopping bags and old clothes. I've decided to let you help me decide whether or not to continue. But first, I want to tell you a story that may help you decide. I heard this story about the Divrei Chaim of Sanz during a talk given by the great Rabbi Shalom Shwadron *ztz"l*."

Then my father told me this story:

Once the Divrei Chaim was traveling with his Chassidim on the main road that led to the city of Sanz. Suddenly, as they passed a certain village, the Chassidim saw Reb Chaim's entire body tremble. Before they could ask him to explain, he commanded the wagon driver to turn the wagon straight into the town.

News of their arrival spread like wildfire and within a few minutes of their arrival in the village, hundreds of people were following behind the wagon, anxious to catch a glimpse of the *tzaddik*'s radiant face.

Reb Chaim told the wagon driver in which direction to go, even though he had never before been in that town. They passed almost all of the main streets, and by now, almost every Jew in town was following the wagon.

All of a sudden, Reb Chaim gave the order to stop.

The people looked at the house next to which the wagon had stopped and their faces turned pale. "The Rebbe must want to bring to task 'Reb

Pesach the Priest' for what happened here two months ago."

Reb Chaim's Chassidim were astonished to hear the strange nickname "Reb Pesach the Priest." Their amazement increased when the villagers told them that Reb Pesach used to be the town's charity collector but that he had been dismissed from his position because of the great *chillul Hashem* he had caused.

The Chassidim tried to prevent the crowd from following the Rebbe into the house of "Reb Pesach the Priest," but to their shock, Reb Chaim said, "To the contrary — let them come."

The Rebbe himself went quickly to the door of Reb Pesach and knocked. Reb Pesach, upon seeing the holy Rebbe at the entrance to his home, almost fainted.

"Wh-what does the Rebbe want from me?" he stammered.

"I want to enter your home to question you about something that is in your house. Please let me do so," the Rebbe commanded.

Reb Pesach was alarmed, but hastened to reply, "If the esteemed Rebbe so wishes, my home is open to him."

The Rebbe entered the house and strode directly into Reb Pesach's bedroom, followed by Reb Pesach and anyone else who was able to squeeze himself in. Reb Pesach was frightened out of his wits and was white as a sheet.

When the Rebbe directed his gaze at the closet that stood in the room, Reb Pesach became even more terrified.

"Open the closet," ordered the Rebbe. Reb Pesach, shaking and trembling, hastened to do as he had been told.

And when he opened the door, what do you think was revealed for all to see? Nothing less than the black garments of a priest!

The Chassidim couldn't believe their eyes. Now they understood the nickname given Reb Pesach by the townspeople.

Yet, how was it possible that a Jew who had served for so many years as the village charity collector because he was considered honest and upright, had the garments of a priest in his house?

Everyone stood there in shock — everyone, that is, except the Rebbe.

What did he do? He hugged Reb Pesach, then clapped him on the back with great affection and turned to his Chassidim.

"Now do you understand why I turned off the main road to go into this town?" he asked. "I smelled the fragrance of *Gan Eden*, and that fragrance pulled me to this town, to this house, to this room, and to this closet.

"Tell me, Reb Pesach, why do these garments have the fragrance of *Gan Eden*?"

All the onlookers were shocked at what they had just heard. How was it possible? A fragrance of *Gan Eden* coming from a priest's clothes?

Then Reb Pesach revealed the whole story to everyone there, and this is what he said:

Every month I make the "mitzvah rounds." By that I mean that I go around the village from door to door collecting money to distribute to the poor. One night, after I had spent the whole day making the rounds and collecting a significant amount of money from the townspeople that I distributed to the poor, a widow came to my home. She was crying and pleading for money to marry off her daughter. At long last a good *shidduch* had been proposed for the girl, but because they didn't have any money, they were unable to go through with it.

The widow's story touched my heart, but I told her straight away that I had just returned from rounds where I had already knocked on all the doors of the village. How could I go around again?

"Who knows the situation of the villagers as well as you," I said to her. "Of rich people, you know there aren't any here. As for everyone else, I've cleaned out practically every last *pruta*, took the money and gave it to the poor. What can I do now? From where can I get more money?"

All my explanations did nothing to calm the

widow, who continued to plead with me. "What will become of my daughter? Must she remain unmarried until the hairs on her head turn white? What will become of me? I lost my husband many years ago and all my hopes are placed in my only daughter. Please help me. Don't send me away empty-handed!"

Deeply troubled, but convinced that there was no way I could help, I shrugged my shoulders and said, "What can I do?"

Suddenly, I had an idea. I remembered one place I still hadn't visited — the town tavern.

It goes without saying that this was the gathering place for all types of lowly people. But, feeling like a condemned man who grasps at a straw, so too I hoped that this woman's salvation would be brought through those same empty men by Hashem.

I stood up and took action. I walked in the direction of the tavern. When I entered the place, the unruly fellows there pounced on me immediately and jeered, "Ho, Reb Pesach, Reb Pesach, money, money. Reb Pesach wants money but does money want Reb Pesach? Ha, ha, ha!"

I stood there facing them and said without shame, "Yes, Reb Pesach wants money, and money wants Reb Pesach — so that an orphaned Jewish girl can get married."

Loud laughter burst from their drunken

mouths. Then suddenly, the son of the *poritz* in the area who had the most money — and the most hatred for Jews — had a brainstorm. He turned to me and said, "You know what? Tell me, *zhid*, how much money do you need?"

I told him the amount needed, two thousand rubles, and then he said to me, "If you do everything I ask of you, I'll give you the entire amount."

I asked him, "What do you want me to do?" with great hope in my voice.

He replied: "Listen, Reb Pesach. If you want those few cents, you'll have to dress up in the clothes of the priest. And not only that, but we'll send you through all the streets of the village wearing those clothes, and we'll take big drums and cymbals and anything else that can make noise so that everyone will come outside to see what's happening. Then everyone will see how you, Reb Pesach with the big beard almost to the ground, are dressed in the priest's clothes. What do you say to that?" he roared to his friends. "Ha, ha, ha, it's a great idea, isn't it?"

He and his friends slapped each other on the back. It was clear to them, just as it was clear to me, that he was asking too much. Would a Jew dare wear the clothes of a priest?

And that's exactly what I said to myself. *Chas v'shalom*! I thought. How could I do such a thing?

How could I, the esteemed Reb Pesach, head of a large family, bring upon myself such shame and humiliation that would be remembered for the rest of my life?

Yet I immediately realized that I wasn't worried about heaven's honor but about my own personal honor. I realized that this was the advice of the *yetzer hara* telling me to refuse to help the poor widow. For, after all, there is no prohibition against wearing black garments that a priest once wore. I said to myself, Because of your own honor an orphan girl shouldn't get married?

I immediately overpowered my *yetzer* and gave my answer.

"Fine," I said, "I am ready for this charade as long as it will help a Jewish daughter stand under the wedding canopy."

The son of the *poritz* jumped at the opportunity and started to drag me by the arm. "Come along with me, *shnorrer*," he sneered, "and I'll dress you in the royal vestments. Ha, ha..."

He and his friends dragged me to the *poritz*'s house and there they forced me to put the priest's garments on over my clothes. Then, after they finished their "work," they dragged me through the entire town, to the accompaniment of the deafening noise made by the "orchestra." Naturally all the Jews in town came out of their homes to see what was going on. At first, they were shocked. Soon, though, they were saying to each other, "What's come over Reb Pesach?" "He's gone completely mad!" "He was always a bit crazy." "Like has found like," and other similar comments.

I had never been so humiliated in my life. Every minute that passed seemed like a year. Tears streamed down my face at the peals of laughter from the drunken bunch of rowdies mingled with the sounds of protest coming from my fellow Jews.

When they finally finished dragging me through town, they let me go home, still wearing the clothes of the priest, humiliated and dejected. For me, it was the hardest "rounds" I had ever made — but I also got the most money. I collected the enormous sum of two thousand rubles, enough to marry off the orphan and support the couple for several years. I decided that all the humiliation had been worth it as long as the widow found happiness and contentment.

Two months have passed since then. The whole town despises me. My fellow Jews are certain that I agreed to do the ugly deed for personal reward. They never dreamed that the money was given in its entirety to the widow, and that the orphan is to be married in another month.

I can't tell you how terrible it is for me. Many

times, when I feel especially sad about what happened, I say to myself, Maybe you shouldn't have done it. But then I open the closet, look at the priest's clothes, and remember that I wore those clothes for Hashem's sake. I know that Hashem will repay me from Above.

No sooner had Reb Pesach finished his story than he burst into heartfelt sobs. Everyone joined in, for they had never in their lives heard a story of such self-sacrifice. Only the Rebbe was still smiling.

"Now do you understand the meaning of that fragrance from *Gan Eden* I smelled from the main road?" he asked. "Now do you know why I followed that fragrance until it led me to this house?"

Then the Rebbe surprised everyone by saying to Reb Pesach, "When the day comes for you to leave this world, ask that they wrap you in these garments, so that they will be an advocate for you."

"That's what the Divrei Chaim, the Rebbe of Sanz, said," my father ended his story, "and so it was. Rabbi Shalom Shwadron ended the story by saying that when the day came and Reb Pesach died, they wrapped him in the priest's garments, and so buried him. The strangest thing of all was that many years later, when they needed to open the grave, they found that Reb Pesach's body had stayed whole. No maggots or worms had touched it, except for one part of his foot that they had forgotten to wrap in the priest's garments, which decayed."

My father looked at me and said, "Now do you understand the great reward of a person who does a mitzvah that involves humiliation? It's no trick to do a regular mitzvah. The trick is to do a mitzvah that's not that comfortable and convenient to do. Are you still ashamed of your father, the moving man and caretaker?"

The answer was obvious, so I only said one thing before I fell asleep: "Abba, next time you go out on a job, it doesn't matter what, with the driver of the pickup truck, don't forget to take me along. Okay?"

We find this idea — that a mitzvah done involving humiliation has a special reward — in the Gemara.

In *Kesubos*, page 17a, it says (in Aramaic, of course): "When Rav Shemuel bar Yitzchak died, a pillar of fire separated him from the rest of the world. Our sages tell us that a pillar of fire only appeared for one or two people in a generation."

Rav Shemuel bar Yitzchak reached this level because he used to dance at weddings and act like a clown to bring more happiness to the bride and groom. We see from this that, despite all the mitzvos he did and all the Torah he learned, and even though he certainly received reward from them, he was given a special reward for allowing himself to be the object of scorn and derision when doing a mitzvah.

Secret Weapon

Eliyahu's Story

Secret Weapon

I live in Jerusalem and go to HaMesorah. I'm an average kid, not too tall and not too short, not too quiet and not too loud. I guess I'm what you'd call "parve."

Recently an old man, actually a very old man, came to live in our neighborhood. He doesn't have his own apartment. Instead, he lives in an old-age home nearby.

He *davens* in our shul and that's how I know him.

Everyone calls him "The Brisker." That's because he likes to tell stories and anecdotes about the Brisk dynasty. From the way he talks, you can see he must be part of the dynasty himself.

Last Shabbos I saw him giving out candies. I ran to stand next to him, of course. I didn't ask for anything, though, because that's not nice. But I knew that if I stood there, I'd get some.

I did.

I looked at my haul, said a nice thank-you, quickly removed a wrapper, made a *berachah*, and — plop, the candy instantly found its place between my tongue and cheek.

My friends did exactly the same thing.

"*Shehakol*," the old man said to us.

"We said it," we chorused.

"But the *berachah* is '*shehakol nihyah bidvaro*.'"

"That's exactly what we said," answered Yirmiyahu.

"Not exactly."

Why not exactly? I thought with irritation. But I didn't say anything. I respect older people.

Shimon said softly, "I'm positive I made a berachah."

"The berachah you all said was not '*shehakol nihyah bidvaro*,'" said the old man.

"So what was it?" we asked, curious.

"'*Ruch ta shem keinu lech lam kol nya ro*,'" recited the old man. "You all swallowed the first part of every word."

We burst out laughing. He had done a perfect imitation of us.

"Again," we asked.

"'*Ruch ta shem keinu lech lam kol nya ro*,'" the

elderly man repeated, exactly the same way.

It was a fantastic imitation. We asked him to do it again, but he said, "First of all, let me tell you a story I heard from the great *mashgiach* Rabbi Dan Segal *shlita*. After that I'll do another imitation. Agreed?"

A story and an imitation too — how could we not agree?

"Sure we agree," we said.

Then he began to tell us this story:

Once upon a time, a Rabbi in Tunis was out walking with two of his students. On the way, they encountered a big, strong Arab who, upon seeing the Rabbi, jumped on him with the intention of killing him.

The two students begged him to leave the rabbi alone, but the Arab warned them that if they didn't move out of his way, he'd kill them too.

"I want to kill your rabbi," he said.

At that moment, the Rabbi said to his students, "Escape and save yourselves."

At first they refused to part from him, but he commanded them to leave, and they did. They walked away with tears in their eyes and then watched from afar to see what would happen.

The Arab prepared to kill the rabbi with his knife but before he did he said, "According to our custom, we must fulfill your last wish. If you have a final request before your death, hurry up and say it."

What do you think the respected Rabbi asked for?

A glass of water.

The Arab was shocked. He never expected a request like that. However, since a custom is a custom, he handed a cup of water to the Rabbi.

The Rabbi looked at the water, said a blessing in a loud, strong voice, *"Baruch attah Hashem, Elokeinu Melech haOlam shehakol nihyah bidvaro,"* and began to drink.

The instant he finished his blessing, an Arab sheik passed by. This sheik was also an infamous Jew-hater, yet when he saw the Arab bandit sharpening his knife, he cried out to him, "Kill all the Jews but don't touch their rabbis!"

The Arab heard him and stopped. He started to look for the two students, but they had run away. The Arab had no choice but to free the Rabbi.

During the *seudas hodayah* the Rabbi held to commemorate his rescue, the students asked him about something that had been puzzling them. "Is it seemly for a rabbi to ask for a drink of water as his final request? Aren't there more important things to do before dying besides having a drink of water?"

"Do you really think I needed a glass of water?" the Rabbi scolded them. "It was the blessing of *shehakol* that I needed!" Then the Rabbi told them that he had a tradition that had been handed down for generations from the Baal Shem Tov that by saying the blessing *shehakol* with deep concentration, evil decrees can be annulled and no creature on earth can harm whoever does so.

"That's the reason I asked for the water," concluded the Rabbi. "So that I could say the blessing *shehakol*."

The old man ended his spell-binding tale and looked at us. I was still captive to the magic of the story, but suddenly I felt that not everything was clear to me.

"What's the connection?" I heard myself ask. "What's the connection between *shehakol* and saving a life?"

"That's a good question," noted the old man. "Bring me a glass of water and I'll answer it."

I ran to bring the water. He took the glass, looked at us, and recited, "*Ruch ta shem keinu lech lam kol na ro.*"

We laughed again, this time at ourselves. Besides what we miss out on every time we say a blessing like that, we saw how we looked and sounded. That old man did a great imitation.

We got the message. Then the old man's smile disappeared. The old man looked at the glass, closed his eyes, and started to say the blessing in the Brisker style, with great intensity and concentration, *"Baruch attah Hashem, Elokeinu Melech haOlam shehakol nihyah bidvaro,"* he recited and drank from the glass of water.

"Rabbi Dan Segal quotes something that is written in the *Nefesh haChaim,* Gate 3," said the old man. "Bring me the *sefer* and I'll read directly from it."

We all ran to look for the *sefer.* Guess who found it? As usual, it was Nechemyah, who's as swift as a deer and who has eyes as sharp as an eagle's.

The old man opened the *sefer* and began to read: "It is truly an important matter and a wonderful *segulah* that can cancel and annul all judgments and other forces against a person so they will have no power over him, and will not have any impact whatsoever — when a person concentrates with his whole heart and says, 'He is the real God and there is none other besides Him.'

"When you don't rely on yourself but instead place your faith in Hashem and say, 'there is none other besides Him,' then Hashem will save you from every misfortune," said the old man. "Think for a minute about the words *'shehakol*

nihyah bidvaro.' Everything that happens in this
world happens only because of Hashem and not
because of anyone else. In other words...?"

"There is none other besides Him," we
chorused.

"And now I'll tell you another story," said the
old man.

"When Rav Chaim of Brisk fled from the
Holocaust together with his close *talmid* Reb
Itze'le Levin, they had to cross the border
between Poland and Lithuania.

"There were many road blocks along the way.
Practically every couple of miles there were
German or Polish soldiers who guarded the
border to prevent Jews from fleeing and to
prevent people from taking their possessions out
with them.

"Now listen to the amazing thing that
happened: Rav Chaim, who fled with most of his
possessions, along with his *talmid* and an entire
group of Jews, who also had all their household
goods with them, passed through all the checkpoints, without anyone bothering them!

"Everything went smoothly until they arrived
at the next to the last checkpoint. Suddenly a
German soldier came over to them and ordered
the group to stand ready for inspection.

"He began to search through the possessions
of Rav Chaim's *talmid*, Reb Itze'le Levin, who

was wretchedly poor. Naturally, he didn't find anything.

"After that, he turned to Rav Chaim's suitcase. This contained valuables, and the punishment for taking them out of the country was death without trial.

"He started to search through the bundle. Reb Itze'le was appalled. He began trembling because he knew what the results of the search would be. He glanced fearfully at Rav Chaim, but Rav Chaim looked quite calm as he murmured something.

"The *talmid* felt as if he were about to faint from fear. The German had already removed the first layer of clothes. Another layer and the treasure would be revealed. He picked up the first piece of clothing and then...

"Just then a German jeep screeched to a stop. The person in it, who appeared to be a high-ranking German officer, shouted at the soldier, 'Leave these Jews and come immediately — we have an important job to do.'

"The soldier immediately left the group, ran to the jeep, and got in. It raced away at top speed.

"Reb Itze'le Levin fainted.

"The rest of the group hurried to revive him. Rav Chaim sat next to him and asked, 'Why were you so terrified?'

" 'The question is, why was the Rabbi so calm?'

" 'I'll tell you,' said Rav Chaim. 'The minute the soldier started to search through my things, the thought arose in me: Why should this be happening to us right now of all times, and not at one of the dozens of checkpoints we went through before? Why did a miracle happen at all those other checkpoints and not here?

" 'And then I remembered,' said Rav Chaim. 'When I left the house on this dangerous journey, I knew there was no way we would be saved in the natural course of events. Therefore I decided to rely on the *segulah* of the *Nefesh HaChaim*, to concentrate continuously on saying, "there is none other besides Him," that everything that happens is only through Hashem's word. And that was the secret of our success at all those other checkpoints.

" 'However,' continued Rav Chaim, 'The minute we reached the final checkpoint, and it looked like we'd get through safely, my mind wandered from thinking about "there is none other besides Him," and I started to think of where we'd go in Poland. That's when the German stopped us. When he finished searching through your baggage and went on to mine, I realized that the reason for this suffering lay with us, and I started to concentrate again deeply on the fact that Hashem and only Hashem runs the world, and that whatever will be, will be according to His word. And then, of course, the jeep came.'

"Now do you understand the importance hidden within the words '*shehakol nihyah bidvaro*'? said the old man.

We didn't answer. The story had a powerful effect on us.

"Did it really happen?" I asked.

"Every single word is true," said the old man.

"How do you know the story?" I asked.

The old man smiled. We could see he was trying to decide whether or not to say. Finally, he decided to tell us.

"My name is Itze'le Levin."

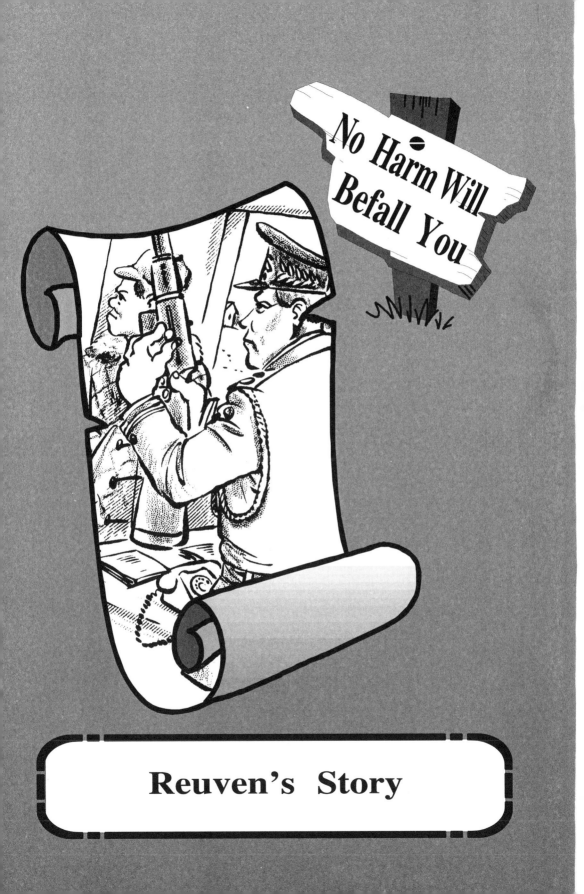

No Harm Will Befall You

Reuven's Story

No Harm Will Befall You

I live in Haifa and I'm in the fourth grade.

One Shabbos morning last year, I went out to play with my friends.

We played next to the yard of the shul. In the middle of the game we got bored and started to swing on the shul's old iron gate.

The gate creaked and squeaked loudly. We were having a lot of fun from the combination of the swinging and the squeaking, so we started to go faster.

Six kids on one old gate — about fifty years old or something — and what happens?

You guessed right. The gate collapsed.

The only think I remember is suddenly falling backwards. My five friends were hanging on the other side of the gate so they fell forward with the gate — right on top of me.

The pain was horrible. The heavy gate was lying on me. The other kids got off fast and tried to lift up the gate. It was really hard, but they did it. I saw their worried faces and suddenly I realized why. I was covered with blood. Every part of my body hurt. I started screaming in pain.

My parents came right away and tried to help me stand up. When my father took my hand, I screamed.

"He must have broken his hand," said my father.

"Try to move it," said a neighbor.

I tried and the terrible pain came back. I could move the other hand.

One neighbor brought water and washed off my face, which was scratched all over. Little by little, I felt stronger, until finally I was able to stand by myself and take a few steps.

The only thing is, my hand was hanging down in a funny way and hurting a lot. I looked at it. My arm was swollen around the wrist. It was obviously a serious break.

A neighbor who knew first aid splinted the break, made a sling with a wide bandage and tied it around my neck. But the pain was still awful.

"There's no choice. We'll have to go to Rothstein," said my father.

Rothstein is the hospital closest to our house, only a ten-minute walk away. We started to walk there.

Even though I had walked that way lots of times before, this time was the hardest of all.

Every move I made hurt, and since Haifa has a lot of hills and steps, there were a lot of moves. I suffered in silence because I knew I had no choice. My father taught me that it didn't pay to cry if you weren't going to get anything from it — except for when you're sad, to get rid of some of the sadness. But I wasn't sad. It just hurt. I had already cried enough, though.

Every difficulty has an end, and so when we got to the entrance of the hospital, I figured that my troubles were over.

I was wrong.

We went to the orthopedics department. A doctor, who talked with a strong Russian accent, checked me and said I needed to have a cast put on. The truth is, I felt a little happy about it. You know, having people sign their names on it and all that. But then, all of a sudden, a nurse came over to my father and said to him, "Please fill out this form and sign it."

"It's Shabbos today," my father said. "We can't sign. I'll sign after Shabbos."

"What kind of business is this?" fumed the nurse. "Everyone signs and you'll sign too!"

My father spoke to her very calmly. "Please try to understand. As Jews we can't sign on Shabbos. It's forbidden."

"If you don't sign, the boy will not be treated," declared the nurse.

I was furious. What a way to act. I looked at my father. His forehead was wrinkled. I saw that he was trying very hard to remain calm. He certainly wasn't feeling calm.

"Excuse me," my father said in a quiet voice, "but I'm not doing this to irritate you. It's just forbidden for us. Do you understand? Forbidden."

"I don't understand a thing," retorted the nurse. "If you sign, he'll be treated. If not..."

My father looked at the doctor, but he just shrugged. "I'm not the one who decides things here," he said. "I only treat whoever she lets me treat." I saw that he really wanted to help but that he was afraid of the nurse. It looked strange to me. A doctor is higher up than a nurse, so why did he have to be afraid? Anyway, he stood there, his eyes showing sympathy for our fate, but all he did was repeat what he'd said about not being able to do anything. "It's not in my realm of authority" — those were his exact words.

My father explained to me that the doctor was probably a new immigrant who was worried about his job.

The nurse went into a room followed by the

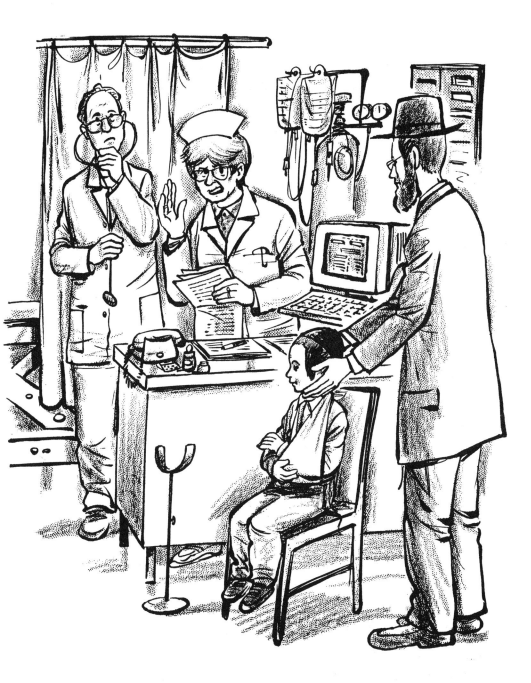

doctor. We heard voices raised in argument, and then afterwards, the nurse's authoritative voice. A minute later she came out and said, "Let me know when you decide to sign."

We sat down. My father sat thinking and then turned to me and said quietly, "Reuven, do you feel like you can't stand the pain any more?"

"Why do you ask?"

"Because there might be an opinion that says we have to sign, even though I don't think it fits our situation exactly. I'd have to check it out." My father spoke out loud, weighing the pros and cons. To my mind, though, the decision was obvious.

"Abba, I really don't want us to sign, no matter what."

My father looked worriedly at my blue, swollen arm and I saw that he was caught between concern for his son and the knowledge that it was forbidden to sign.

The nurse stood there staring at us. My father looked at me and then said to her, "You are endangering your job. You are preventing a boy who is suffering, from getting treatment. This will not pass unreported."

"I'm not afraid of you," said the nurse. "As far as I'm concerned, all of you can leave."

"What did she mean by 'all of you'?" I asked my father. "There's only you and me here."

"She meant all the Jews who keep Torah and mitzvos," my father explained. He didn't need to say more. Most of the people who live in Haifa don't keep Torah and mitzvos, and lots of times kids and even adults say not nice things to us. More than once I've been insulted for no good reason by a kid or teenager without a *kippa*. I never understood the reason for this hatred but I got used to it. My father used to explain to me that I should pity them and not get angry. That's what I did.

But this nurse wasn't having any pity on me. She looked at us angrily, as if we were doing something bad to her.

The doctor stood and watched, too. In his eyes you could see that he didn't agree with what she was doing, but he didn't dare go against her.

"We'll wait here until after Shabbos is over," my father said.

The nurse answered, "As far as I'm concerned you can wait here until his hand swells like a...like a..." She caught herself and stopped talking.

I never saw my father so angry. But he held himself back, and instead of shouting at the nurse the way she wanted him to, he said aloud as if to no one in particular, "What a compassionate nurse..."

You could see that what he said made her

really angry. She started yelling at my father and at all religious people and their rabbis. I didn't hear the exact words because my father went to the trouble of plugging up my ears with two fingers. It was important to him that I not hear the nurse's words of blasphemy.

I burst out crying. I was so hurt. Why does she hate us like that? I wondered. What did we ever do to her? She doesn't even know us.

The nurse stopped shouting and left. My father took me over to a corner and tried to calm me down.

"A believing Jew has to withstand tests," he said. "What does the whole world have against the Jew? What do those who throw off the yoke of their faith have against the religious Jew? Is there any explanation for it?

"There's only one explanation: Jealousy. They're just jealous of us, Reuven. You have to understand that it's nothing more than simple envy of the good and peaceful life we have, of our simple trust and faith in Hashem. They have nothing to hold on to in times of trouble. We do. They don't believe that there is Someone above that a person can pray to Who watches over everyone. Is it any wonder they're jealous?"

From the corner of my eye I saw the doctor sit down on a nearby chair. I heard him sigh. I whispered to my father, "Is it dangerous for my hand to stay this way until after Shabbos?"

My father didn't answer right away, but then he declared, "No. I'm not worried at all. Just now I remembered a story that reminds me of what's happening here. It's a story I heard from my father, may he rest in peace, about the Admor of Machnovke. It's a story that teaches us that 'one who keeps a mitzvah will come to no harm.' Sit quietly and listen."

I noticed that the doctor had also pricked up his ears.

"You surely know that until only a few years ago it was forbidden for Jews in Russia to live as Jews are supposed to live. Anyway, many Jews continued to keep the mitzvos despite the terrible conditions.

"The Admor of Machnovke *ztz"l* was one of them, and since he was a leader, the government dealt with him very strictly and followed his every move. Time after time they would grab him, put him on trial, and send him to spend a few years in Siberia as punishment. But each time he would come back in a miraculous way to continue spreading, with great self-sacrifice, Hashem's Torah amongst his fellow Jews.

"One of the times he was to be punished, the Admor was summoned to headquarters to fill in details of his identity. It was a law that after seven days of labor an accounting of the prisoner and his actions had to be written down. This statement had to be signed by the prisoner.

"It was Shabbos," I piped up.

"Exactly."

"When the Admor was asked to sign the report, he refused adamantly, saying, 'Today is Shabbos.'

"The official was enraged. 'Sign, I said!' he thundered.

"The official was boiling mad and ordered the prisoner to come with him to General Potshnik, the camp's commander, who was famous for being the best marksman in the entire Russian army.

"The General looked at the Rebbe and ordered: 'Sign immediately. Otherwise you'll face a bitter end.'

"The Rebbe answered, 'It's Shabbos today, and he who keeps the mitzvos will come to no harm.'

"The general was filled with uncontrollable rage. 'Sign! If not, I'll kill you,' he said. The Rabbi stood firm. It was a *gezeras shemad*, and so fell in the category of 'let yourself be killed rather than transgress.'

" 'Go right ahead and kill me,' said the rabbi. 'I will not desecrate the Sabbath.'

"The general turned red with rage. He clicked the trigger of his famous rifle and roared at the Rabbi, 'You insolent Jew! How dare you speak to me that way?'

"Yet the Rabbi was not alarmed and answered quietly, 'If I'm not mistaken, you are Jewish too, aren't you? Potshnik is a Jewish name. When I was a child I knew a blacksmith by that name. Was he your father?'

"This was too much for the general. Not only was the Rabbi refusing to obey him, but he was also reminding him of the fact that he was Jewish, a fact he wanted to forget. He lifted his gun. Despite there being practically no distance between them, he closed one eye, as do all sharpshooters, and aimed straight at the Rabbi, who stood without blinking an eye.

"He fired the rifle..."

My father interrupted his story. I watched his mouth, waiting to hear what happened next. The doctor did the same thing.

"...and the official who had reported the Rabbi to the general fell down dead," said my father.

"Everyone present stood in shock. They had never seen anyone 'succeed' in missing like that, let alone the best marksman in the entire Russian army.

"The general was stunned. He realized that the man standing before him must be a holy man. He trembled and did a complete about-face. He humbly asked the Rabbi's forgiveness for the way he had acted and then said, 'Yes, Rabbi, I too am a Jew. Tell me what you lack. Soon it will be

Rosh Hashanah. Do you need something for the holiday?'

" 'Yes,' answered the Rabbi. 'I need a shofar.'

"It took a lot of effort, but eventually the general managed to bring the Rabbi an excellent shofar for Rosh Hashanah.

"Within the year, the general saw to it that the Rabbi was released to Buchara, from where he returned to Russia, to spread Hashem's Torah to his fellow Jews," my father concluded his story.

Silence descended on the gloomy hospital corridor. I was thinking about the brave and holy Rabbi. Suddenly I felt very proud that I was acting the same way. Suddenly I didn't care about the pain in my hand. It lost all meaning for me. Then I remembered that I had wanted to ask my father something.

"What happened to the general?"

"They say he continued serving in the army but from that day on, he decided to take it upon himself to help every Jew who came to the camp. They say that in the end, the government caught him. Till this very day, no one knows his fate."

This ending made me a little sad because I wanted to hear that the general became religious and lived happily ever after, like lots of stories end. But what can you do? Real stories don't always end the way you want.

All of a sudden I heard the doctor start

talking. "Go into the room. I'm putting on a cast for you."

We looked at him in astonishment. He repeated, "Go ahead inside. It's okay. I'll make a cast. I'm not afraid of that nurse."

We looked at him. My father took hold of my good hand and led me into the room.

The doctor started to dip cloths in water to prepare the cast for me. First he covered my arm in a strange kind of cotton. Then suddenly...

The nurse walked in.

"Did they sign?" she asked.

"No."

"By whose authority are you treating them?"

"My own," he answered firmly. "Get it?"

"You know, you're new here, on a trial period. I'll make sure you're not hired permanently."

"Listen, I'm not afraid of you," answered the doctor. "You can do what you want. Even if you take a rifle and... The Rebbe of Machnovke said that whoever keeps a mitzvah, nothing bad will happen to him."

We looked at him with admiration. We knew from where he was getting his courage.

"What's going on here? Did you suddenly decide to become a Jew?" the nurse said sarcastically.

"I *am* a Jew, and that can never be changed," the doctor said.

"But until now all you talked about was how you weren't even sure you were Jewish. You said your grandfather was some kind of general in the Russian army. So why are you suddenly deciding that you are Jewish?"

The doctor finished putting on the cast. His hand smoothed the wet bandages that were starting to dry and harden. We looked at him. We watched as he removed his rubber gloves, took an identity card out of his pocket, opened it before our eyes, and said with feeling, "It's become clear to me beyond the shadow of a doubt that Potshnik is a Jewish name."

Glossary

The following glossary provides a partial explanation of some of the Hebrew and Yiddish words used in this book. It reflects the way the specific word is used herein. There may be alternate spellings and meanings for the words.

Baruch Hashem: thank God
berachah: blessing
chalaka: traditional first haircut for boys at the age of three
chas v'chalilah or *chas v'shalom*: heaven forbid!
cheder: Talmud Torah, school for young boys
chevra'man: popular
chillul Hashem: desecration of God's Name
gedolei hador: Torah leaders of the generation
gezeras shemad: decree of forced apostasy
Hashem: God
hishtadlus: effort
kever: grave
Kosel: Western Wall
lashon hara: slander
mashgiach: spiritual advisor
Mashiach: the Messiah
mesader kiddushin: the person who performs the marriage ceremony
nachas (Y.): satisfaction
Navi: Prophets
poritz: non-Jewish landowner
Rosh Chodesh: the beginning of the Jewish month
Rosh Kollel: dean of a *kollel*, a yeshiva for married students
Rosh Yeshiva: dean of a yeshiva
sefer: sacred book
segulah: talisman
seudas hodayah: festive meal of thanksgiving
shalom aleichem: Peace be unto you!
shidduch: proposal of marriage
shiur: lesson
talmid(im): student(s)
tefillah: prayer
teshuvah: repentance
tzaddik: pious, righteous person
tzedakah: charity
yetzer hara: evil inclination
z'chus: merit